"From Prohibition and Hawley-Smoot to ethanol and Fann[...] ernmental economic fiascoes mounts to a vertiginous climax of decades of deficits in Burton Abrams's wise and uproarious *The Terrible 10*. A must-read for muddled millennials, U.S. Senators, high school teachers, Federal Reserve governors, and all lovers of liberal follies and conservative crony capitalism."

—**George Gilder**, author of *Knowledge and Power: The Information Theory of Capitalism and How It Is Revolutionizing our World, Wealth and Poverty, Telecosm, Microcosm*, and *The Silicon Eye*

"*The Terrible 10* clearly and superbly identifies and discusses in detail the ten worst government policy disasters of the past ten decades. The book is a delight to read, interweaving economics and politics with history and not shying away from the naming of names. Each disaster resulted from unrealistic objectives, ignorance, near-sightedness, the abuse of power, and/or special-interest group manipulation, and the book provides much needed lessons for the future."

—**James D. Gwartney**, Professor of Economics and Director, Stavros Center for the Advancement of Free Enterprise and Economic Education, Florida State University

"*The Terrible 10* is a book that's both delightful and therapeutic. In wry and stylish prose Burton Abrams describes all the symptoms of what happens when the disease of government infects the body of the marketplace. And Abrams has the macro-economic cure. Legislators need to cut down on the saturated fat of entitlements, start doing more exercise of regulatory restraint, and consume less ideological junk food. *The Terrible 10* will help us restore the balance of our economy's health away from politics and toward liberty."

—**P.J. O'Rourke**, bestselling author of *Parliament of Whores, Eat the Rich, Don't Vote: It Just Encourages the Bastards*, and other books

"Most bad economic policies are like zombies: they keep coming back to life. But some economic follies never even die, living eternally in the philosophy of both political parties. The excellent book *The Terrible 10* is a vivid reminder that the fight for freedom is a tough one, and it does, indeed, require 'eternal vigilance.'"

—**Véronique de Rugy**, Senior Research Fellow, Mercatus Center

"*The Terrible 10* is fascinating, well written, and witty, making it both informative and entertaining. Burton Abrams's superb account of his ten most terrible government programs makes reading this book time well spent for everyone."

—**Thomas R. Saving**, Jeff Montgomery Professor of Economics and Director of the Private Enterprise Research Center, Texas A&M University

"The decimation of Americans' economic liberties did not occur in a single stroke. Nor can the blame be entirely laid upon the steps of the Supreme Court. *The Terrible 10: A Century of Economic Folly*, weaves a rich historical narrative to shine light on the combination of political forces behind policies that sound like good ideas on the surface but instead cause undeniable waste and injustice. Burton Abrams tells a engaging tale, and his book is perfect for any reader who cares about liberty and prosperity."

> —**Edward J. Lopez**, BB&T Distinguished Professor of Capitalism, Western
> Carolina University; co-author, *Madmen, Intellectuals, and Academic
> Scribblers: The Economic Engine of Political Change*

"In *The Terrible 10*, Burton Abrams does a wonderful job of explaining why misguided government policies are enacted and describing the costs they have imposed on Americans. This book is both a solid piece of economic analysis as well as fascinating reading thanks to the stories and anecdotes that illustrate the negative consequences of faulty policies."

> —**Randall G. Holcombe**, DeVoe Moore Professor of Economics,
> Florida State University

"*The Terrible 10* is an incisive historical book using both benefit-cost and distributional analyses to identify the 20th century's worst policy consequences. From Prohibition to environmental regulation to macroeconomic policy, Burton Abrams couples engaging narrative with evidence and economic analysis to illuminate the large costs of economic policy mistakes. He also identifies some of the causes and incentives underlying these outcomes. Can we learn from this history and avoid making such policy mistakes in the future?"

> —**L. Lynne Kiesling**, Distinguished Senior Lecturer, Department of
> Economics, Northwestern University

"Selecting from the countless good candidates Uncle Sam's ten worst policy failures is a Herculean task. But Burton Abrams pulls it off splendidly in *The Terrible 10*! Yet more impressive is the clarity and conciseness that Prof. Abrams marshals to give his case striking credence. Even the likes of *New York Times* editorialists will be hard pressed to challenge his arguments. Refuting these arguments will prove nearly impossible."

> —**Donald J. Boudreaux**, Professor of Economics, George Mason University

"*The Terrible 10* is a sobering look at the most destructive government policy blunders of the past 100 years that have hindered growth and undermined liberty."

> —**Daniel J. Mitchell**, Senior Fellow, Cato Institute

THE TERRIBLE
10

The INDEPENDENT INSTITUTE

THE INDEPENDENT INSTITUTE is a non-profit, non-partisan, scholarly research and educational organization that sponsors comprehensive studies in political economy. Our mission is to boldly advance peaceful, prosperous, and free societies, grounded in a commitment to human worth and dignity.

Politicized decision-making in society has confined public debate to a narrow reconsideration of existing policies. Given the prevailing influence of partisan interests, little social innovation has occurred. In order to understand both the nature of and possible solutions to major public issues, The Independent Institute adheres to the highest standards of independent inquiry, regardless of political or social biases and conventions. The resulting studies are widely distributed as books and other publications, and are debated in numerous conference and media programs. Through this uncommon depth and clarity, the Independent Institute is redefining public debate and fostering new and effective directions for government reform.

100 Swan Way, Oakland, California 94621-1428, U.S.A.
Telephone: 510-632-1366 • Facsimile: 510-568-6040 • Email: info@independent.org • www.independent.org

THE TERRIBLE

10

A CENTURY
OF ECONOMIC
FOLLY

BURTON A. ABRAMS

The INDEPENDENT
INSTITUTE

Oakland, California

The Independent Institute
100 Swan Way, Oakland, CA 94621-1428
Telephone: 510-632-1366
Fax: 510-568-6040
Email: info@independent.org
Website: www.independent.org

Library of Congress Cataloging-in-Publication Data

Abrams, Burton A.
   The terrible 10 : a century of economic folly / Burton A. Abrams.
      pages cm
   Includes bibliographical references and index.
   ISBN 978-1-59813-141-3 (hardcover : alk. paper) — ISBN 978-1-59813-142-0 (pbk. : alk. paper)
1. United States—Economic policy--20th century. 2. United States—Economic conditions—20th century. 3. United States—Social conditions—20th century. 4. United States—Politics and government—20th century. I. Title.
   HC106.A334 2013
   330.973'091—dc23   2013019197

Cover Design: Keith Criss
Cover Image: © iStockphoto/Peter Zelei
Interior Design and Composition by Leigh McLellan Design

Contents

Dedication

For Joni and Karen

Acknowledgments

ALEXANDER TABARROK, RESEARCH DIRECTOR of the Independent Institute, and Roy M. Carlisle, its Acquisitions Director, worked closely with me on this project. Alex read every chapter and provided detailed comments that surely helped to improve the product. Roy supported the project throughout the process and greatly helped with suggestions and strategic planning. Russell Settle originally planned to co-author the project but dropped out for various personal reasons. He wrote the first drafts for the Social Security and Prohibition chapters and read and commented on many of the other chapters. Russ is one of the best economists I've ever known, and his comments were extremely useful.

A large number of people, including noneconomist friends and relatives, read various chapters and alerted me to sections that were unclear or too complicated. My economics colleagues who read and critiqued chapters include David Black, James Butkiewicz, Stacie Beck, Eleanor Craig, William Gehrlein, Will Harris, Bert Levin, James O'Neill, and George Parsons. I would also like to thank several anonymous referees provided by the Independent Institute for their helpful comments. Friends and relatives contributing include Dick and Sally Lybeck, Bob and Doris Earl, Bob and Helen Ahlbrecht, Larry Miller, Charlotte Neigh, Karen Venezky, and my sister, Joni Abrams. Karen and Joni have been my two biggest supporters, and I dedicate this book to them. Finally I thank the Independent Institute and its President, David Theroux, for all their good work in promoting individual liberty and for bringing this project into print. Any remaining deficiencies are my responsibility.

Introduction

THE ECONOMIC PERFORMANCE of the U.S. economy in the twentieth century was an incredible success story. In 1900, the average American earned $5,500 (in year 2010 dollars), and we ranked fourth among all countries in per capita income. By the year 2000, the average American earned about $29,500, and we stood at the summit of economic development. In contrast, the United Kingdom, which started the century in first place, dropped to twelfth by 2000. To paraphrase Frank Sinatra, for the United States, it was not merely a very good year but a very good century. The record could have been better still.

This book focuses not on the good economic policies that helped create the U.S. success story but rather on the policies that were major economic blunders. As former British Prime Minister Winston Churchill noted, those who fail to learn from history are doomed to repeat it. Reflecting on the painful lessons of history not only helps us to avoid repeating them, but constitutes an important first step toward finding solutions for lingering problems. Some of the worst economic policies of the past one hundred years are recent and will continue to create problems for us as we go further into the twenty-first century.

Criteria for Selecting the Worst Economic Policies

How were the ten worst economic policies selected? Two standard economic tools were used. One tool is benefit-cost analysis, which provides a framework for evaluating the social benefits and costs of public policies. The second tool is an equity or fairness assessment. How does the policy impact members of society? Are the distributional consequences fair?

For the most part, the policies chosen either have imposed significantly more costs than benefits on society or have distributional effects that most people would consider unfair. Some of the policies selected satisfy both criteria. It was difficult to winnow the list of bad policies down to the ten worst. Some economists may feel some great candidates were overlooked or the rankings were out of order. Most, however, would agree that the ten selected here were poorly designed and needlessly wasteful.

Why So Many Bad Policies?

Bad economic policies are not hard to find. Some of the worst are old, and some are new; some are Red and some are Blue. Bad economic policies are not the monopoly of any one political party. The blunders divide fairly equally among Democrats and Republicans. This was not the author's intention. Basic forces work to encourage the production of wasteful economic policies, regardless of the political party in power.

Government is plagued by the same governance problems corporations face, arguably more so. Voters elect representatives, and shareholders elect corporate decision-makers, and both groups of owners—voters and shareholders—share the problem of getting their representatives to act responsibly in their behalf. The bigger the corporation and the bigger the government, it would seem, the bigger the governance problem.

When Willie Sutton, one of the most notorious twentieth-century criminals, was asked why he robbed banks, he replied, "because that's where the money is." The same rationale motivates many of those who seek to run large corporations or to hold government office. Government office seekers might honestly add, "because that's also where the power is." Another major problem facing both shareholders and voters is how to keep people like Willie Sutton—or imprisoned financier Bernie Madoff, for that matter—from becoming our corporate and government leaders and how to prevent good, honest corporate and government leaders from evolving into Willie Suttons. Interestingly, two of our wrecks are government Ponzi-type schemes similar to the one operated by Bernie Madoff, only bigger: the pay-as-you-go Social Security and Medicare programs.[1]

---

1. These are not "true" Ponzi schemes, as explained later.

Government governance is in many ways more problem-prone than running a corporation. Shareholders have a common interest, the bottom line, and the failure of executives to perform is eventually clear. Bankruptcy or hostile takeovers are possible consequences for nonperformance in the business world, but these remedies for mismanagement really don't exist in our political market. First, it is often difficult to assign blame for bad economic policies. Most voters are disgusted with Congress, but they may feel their own representatives and senators are doing a good job. Second, replacing Republicans with Democrats or vice versa, which might seem to be a type of hostile takeover, seems to do little to improve governance. Regardless of party, government decision makers tend to favor short-run benefits for friends—especially major campaign contributors and special-interest groups—while imposing costs on the rest of us or imposing the costs on later generations.

When corporate governance fails, as demonstrated by the collapse of such firms as Enron and Lehman Brothers, jobs are lost. Paradoxically, when government governance fails, the role and scope of government is usually increased. For example, the recent failure of government regulation of the financial sector, one of the blunders discussed in this book, produced proposals for not one but two new financial regulatory agencies and a coordinating council to add to the numerous regulatory agencies already in place, agencies that had already demonstrated failure in their assigned tasks.

The Sarbanes-Oxley Act of 2002 was government's attempt to improve corporate governance by reducing accounting abuses and making the bottom line more accurate and transparent. Whether or not Sarbanes-Oxley achieves its objectives, making corporations more accountable and transparent are moves in the right direction. The same reasoning could be applied to government as well. How are we to get the government to impose similar laws regarding its own behavior? This is like asking the fox to set the rules for watching the hen house. Can government governance be improved? This important question is addressed in the epilogue.

Motivating Factors Producing Bad Economic Policies

Governments produce wasteful or ineffective policies for several major reasons:

Special-Interest Groups

Many bad public policies stem from the pressure that special-interest groups place on the political system as they seek to redistribute income or wealth to themselves from others. They seek *legislative profits*, increased profits that come from government subsidies, changes in regulation, or special legislation. *Economic profits* arise from building a better mousetrap or producing more efficiently, but legislative profits are usually characterized by waste.

Special-interest economic policies that are adopted and survive for any significant period tend to have two characteristics. First, the members of the special-interest group stand to gain a substantial amount, so they will fight hard to get and keep it. Of course, they will be willing to share some of that gain with supportive politicians (for example, through campaign contributions). Second, the group paying for these special-interest benefits is large so that no individual feels a substantial burden. Indeed, many of those who pay the bill for special-interest group benefits are often completely unaware of what's happening.

An example will help illustrate the point. Suppose dairy farmers successfully lobby a government for a law that sets milk prices one-cent per quart higher than the market price. A large dairy farmer supplying one million gallons of milk per year would stand to rake in an extra $40,000 annually. By contrast, the typical milk-drinking family will pay just a few pennies more a week for milk, an amount so small that it will generally go unnoticed. This story and numbers have a basis in reality. In 1972, the government raised the price it was guaranteeing dairy farmers for their output. The price of a quart of milk increased by an estimated one cent as a result. The overall gain in revenues to the dairy industry was placed at $500 million per year. When this type of asymmetry in benefits and costs occurs, the situation is ripe for abuse, and bad policies are the result. Some examples discussed in this book include the Hawley-Smoot Act of 1930, which involved tariff legislation supporting domestic producers, and U.S. government regulatory policies in the financial sector that contributed heavily to the Great Recession.

Maternalism/Paternalism/Parentalism

Parents know quite well the need to occasionally restrain the behavior of their children. Paternalism, maternalism, or parentalism applies the power of the state to enact policies that restrain individuals from engaging in activities that lawmakers or their constituents find offensive. Some politically influential pressure group may support the policy, or it even may receive broad support from the electorate. Often the support for such policies is based on ideology or religion and the supporters usually receive only psychological benefits from knowing that their fellow citizens are doing the "right" things. Prohibition, one of the blunders in this book, probably is best described as a paternalistic policy. The government's policies to greatly expand home ownership, fostering the real estate bubble prior to the Great Recession, also could be characterized as paternalistic, although special-interest groups benefited as well.

Majority Takes Advantage

Another reason for bad policies is that the political system, responding to the wishes of the majority, takes advantage of a minority, sometimes imposing substantial costs on them. Overall costs of a policy may exceed the benefits by a wide margin. But as long as the benefits to the majority exceed their costs, such a policy can survive. A highly progressive income tax system that attempts to soak the rich is a good example. A period of incredibly high marginal tax rates on the wealthy is included in the chapter, "Tax Follies." The exemptions and deductions within the tax codes, also dealt with in that chapter, might best be classified as special-interest favors, but paternalism plays a role as well.

Short-run Obsession (Immediosis)

Immediacs are individuals obsessed with immediate gratification with little or no regard for the future consequences of their actions.[2] Politics seems to breed or attract immediacs. Politicians naturally are concerned about getting reelected, and to assist in their reelection, they need to produce tangible benefits for constituents prior to the next election. Policies that offer clear short-run benefits may be adopted, even though the policy's costs outweigh its benefits over the long run.

---

2. This concept is original to the author. Don't expect to find it in Wikipedia—at least, not yet. *Immediosis* is my name for the psychological disorder.

Social Security provides a good example. Between 1968 and 1974, our elected federal officials raised Social Security benefits five separate times, four of them falling during an election year. Overall, benefits were increased 90 percent in this six-year period. Clearly, the large and growing elderly population must have felt very warmly toward the incumbents who showered them with this largesse. Yet, at the time, it was clear that this largesse would create serious problems decades later, as the retiree population grew ever larger. The politicians increasing benefits chose not to worry about the long run, which would be some other elected officials' problem many years down the road. "Short-run gain, long-term pain" is the politician's golden rule for reelection. Four of the ten blunders fall into this category. In addition to Social Security, excessive deficit spending in the first decades of this century receives a chapter. A third is the business cycle engineered by President Richard Nixon that window-dressed the economy before his reelection bid and produced a decade of inflation that required three recessions to correct. Fourth and last is the government's establishment of massive amounts of unfunded obligations, mostly in our Medicare program.

Policymaker Ignorance

Bad economic policies also may arise out of just plain ignorance. Policymakers may think that an idea is superficially sound, unaware of or unable to understand its deeper ramifications. One of the most costly of the wrecks in this book is probably best explained by policymaker ignorance about how the economy functions: the Federal Reserve Bank's mishandling of monetary policy that produced the Great Depression.

Plausible Acceptability

Regardless of the underlying reason for their existence, most bad economic policies have a ring of "plausible acceptability," which helps to diffuse objections from injured parties. Borrowing from Richard Nixon, we might dub this requirement the "Will it play in Peoria?" principle. Consider just a few examples. Tariffs on imports "protect hard-working American workers from cheap foreign labor and unfair competition," their proponents might say—overlooking the damage done to consumers. Prospective homeowners "need subsidies to achieve the American dream," others may argue. These policies would be much less palatable to the American public if the lawmakers said, for example, that tariff protections and mortgage subsidies were supported by special-interest groups that made huge campaign contributions to key politicians. The Hawley-Smoot Act, one of our wrecks, pandered to special interests and started a worldwide trade war. Subsidies given to homeowners to buy houses they couldn't afford are included in the chapter on Tax Follies and in the chapter on the Great Recession.

Let's now turn to identifying and explaining the ten worst policies. Arranging the worst policies in chronological order made sense as it helps to maintain an historical context. I took some liberty in deviating from a strict chronological order. One of the great economic wrecks, for example, owes its origin to legislation passed in 1913, but I plunked it down in the 1950s, when its effects really began to become wasteful. First up is a policy that many readers may not consider an economic policy. It was an attempt to destroy a particular market in the United States, a declaration of war on alcohol. It was the 18th Amendment.

1

Prohibition

The War on Booze

"No tendency is quite so strong in human nature as the desire
to lay down rules of conduct for other people."
  —*William Howard Taft*, 27th president of the United States

"Doubts raced through my mind as I considered the feasibility
of enforcing a law which a majority of honest citizens didn't
seem to want."
  —*Eliot Ness*, agent in the Bureau of Prohibition

THE RADOSEVICH BROTHERS finally had arrived, part of the
nearly half-million immigrants that poured into the United States in 1900, lured
by good jobs, even for those who could barely speak English. They migrated
to Michigan's Upper Peninsula and from there into the northern Minnesota
wilderness, where a newly discovered iron range promised even better opportunities for those willing to work hard. And hard work it was. And there were
the mosquitoes in summer and the bitter cold in winter. The brothers stayed
in a boarding house in Bovey, a small, rowdy mining town of several hundred
immigrants from southern and eastern Europe. The brothers saved their money
and watched Bovey grow with the open-pit mine. After six years in the mines,
they decided to pool their resources and enter the second-biggest growth industry in the region: the sale and distribution of alcohol. The Radosevich Brothers
European Saloon was born, and business boomed.

Virtually nonexistent in 1900, Bovey had grown to a population of 1,377 in
1910. It had thirty saloons, about one for every forty-five inhabitants, possibly a

national record. A mere one hundred yards down the dirt road was the town of Coleraine, a community designed and constructed by the mining company for the mine's white-collar workers. In the northern states, few towns adjacent to each other could have differed more. Coleraine's single-family homes, overlooking Trout Lake, were built on spacious lots. Its residents were well-educated and second- or third-generation Americans. Bovey consisted primarily of tar-papered buildings packed onto small lots. Nearly everyone in Bovey was first-generation with little formal education and few English skills. Bovey was inhabited by immigrants with colorful nicknames like "Switchman," "Jim, the Turk," "Big Dan," and "Pollock." Coleraine was heavily Protestant, "dry," and home to Mr. John C. Greenway, supervisor of the mine. The contrast between Bovey and Coleraine mirrored a divide that was widening in the nation as a whole. But the Radosevich Brothers' Saloon (shown in Figure 1.1) boomed along with the town and the production of iron ore, until 1920 when the saloon's doors were closed permanently by force of law.

On January 16, 1920, after decades of effort, temperance crusaders finally succeeded in getting the manufacture, transportation, and sale of alcoholic beverages in the United States outlawed through the 18th Amendment to the

Figure 1.1. Radosevich Brothers European
Saloon, circa 1910, Bovey, Minnesota.
Photo courtesy of Elizabeth Shoberg.

Constitution. Known as Prohibition or the "noble experiment," the period when the Amendment was in effect would last fourteen years.

Prohibition was a paternalistic/maternalistic law, reflecting the desire of a minority of Americans to impose their views of morality and the proper lifestyle on the majority. It was government-imposed morality. The effort failed miserably. In hindsight, most Americans—and especially those who lived through it—probably view Prohibition as a bizarre, foolish, and even dangerous experiment: a massive, precedent-setting governmental intervention in personal freedom, a waste of our national resources, a loss of an important source of tax revenues, a boon to criminals, a corrupting influence on public officials, and an encouragement to otherwise law-abiding citizens to disregard and disrespect the law. Prohibition produced many more costs than benefits and clearly belongs among the worst economic interventions of the last one hundred years.

How Did It Happen?

In the early 1900s, rural Americans, most of them Protestant, were feeling their way of life threatened. Rural interests controlled the state and national legislatures,[1] and rural concerns often received far more attention politically than did urban concerns. Society was changing in ways that did not meet the approval of people in the rural areas of the country. The nation's population was expanding rapidly, but not evenly. Between 1900 and 1920, the urban population soared by 80 percent, while the rural population grew by a mere 13 percent. By 1917 a majority of U.S. citizens, for the first time in history, lived in cities. Cities offered easy access to saloons, liquor, prostitutes, gambling, and other social features that rural Protestants felt were challenging their values.

---

1. The one-person one-vote rule did not become law in the United States until the 1960s, so rural political interests could control a legislature, even though urban voters outnumbered rural voters by substantial margins. Prior to the U.S. Supreme Court ruling in 1962, in *Baker v. Carr,* districts for state legislatures were based on geography, not population. Thus, before 1962, a rural minority could elect a supermajority of state legislators. The Supreme Court ruling noted that by the early 1960s, two-thirds of all state senators represented only one-third of the population, and two-thirds of all state House members represented 40 percent of the state population.

Another challenge to rural Protestant values came from the waves of new immigrants, like the Radosevich brothers, arriving on U.S. shores. Between 1900 and 1920, 15 million immigrants arrived, increasing the U.S. population by about 16 percent. Between 1900 and 1914, about 75 percent of the immigrants came from central, eastern, and southern Europe—countries like Germany, Italy, and Russia where alcohol consumption was an accepted part of the culture. Most were Roman Catholic and other denominations not Protestant.

Another threat came from alcohol and the problems that were seen to surround its use. In the first decade of the century, alcohol consumption rose rapidly. To accommodate all this drinking, saloons were springing up by the tens of thousands, largely in the cities. Several cities had thousands of saloons. As early as 1906, Chicago reportedly had about 8,500 liquor outlets: roughly one for every one hundred adult males, who at that time were the principal patrons.

The saloon business was highly competitive. In an effort to attract business, many encouraged prostitution and gambling and sold booze to minors. Saloons often stayed open on Sunday in violation of local "blue laws"[2] and saloons were seen as a prime reason for the growing problem of public drunkenness. And they helped to separate wayward husbands from their paychecks, yet another threat to family life. As the 1920s approached, millions viewed saloons as a blight on the American landscape, even many who firmly opposed Prohibition.

Prohibitionists offered other rationales in support of their cause. Prohibition crusaders claimed many positive benefits would flow from Prohibition. The remarks by U.S. Representative Richmond Hobson (D-Alabama) on the House floor in 1914 are illustrative.[3] In support of the temperance movement, he claimed:

> Science has thus demonstrated that alcohol is a . . . poison, poisoning all living things; that alcohol is a habit-forming drug that shackles millions . . . and maintains slavery in our midst; that it lowers in a fearful way the standard of efficiency of the Nation, reducing enormously the

---

2. Blue laws impose some type of religious mandate or observation (e.g., closing businesses on Sundays, etc.).

3. "Richmond Hobson Argues for Prohibition," Schaffer Library of Drug Policy, retrieved from http://www.druglibrary.org/schaffer/alcohol/hobson.htm.

national wealth, entailing startling burdens of taxation, encumbering the public with the care of crime, pauperism, and insanity; that it corrupts politics and public servants, corrupts the Government, corrupts the public morals, lowers terrifically the average standard of character of the citizenship, and undermines the liberties and institutions of the Nation; that it undermines and blights the home and the family, checks education, attacks the young when they are entitled to protection, undermines the public health, slaughtering, killing, and wounding our citizens many fold times more than war, pestilence, and famine combined; that it blights the progeny of the Nation, flooding the land with degenerates . . . .

Prohibitionists emphasized the supposed public health benefits of prohibition. Reduced drinking of alcohol would, they claimed, reduce the incidence of serious illnesses, especially cirrhosis. It would cut down on accidents, a growing problem in the rapidly expanding industrial workplace. It would improve productivity and reduce absenteeism, thereby contributing to the nation's prosperity. Irving Fisher, the well-respected University of Chicago economist, wrote:

Since scientific research has shown that alcoholic beverages slow down the human machine, and since the human machine is the most important machine in industry, we should expect the use of alcoholic beverages to slow down industry, and we should expect Prohibition, if enforced, to speed up industry.[4]

The alleged improvement in labor productivity convinced several leading U.S. industrialists, including John D. Rockefeller, to support Prohibition, at least in its early years.[5] The Prohibition crusaders also argued that Prohibition—especially closing the saloons—would reduce crime, another growing problem, particularly in the cities. Reducing crime would, they claimed, greatly reduce the tax burden created by the growing prison population.

---

4. Irving Fisher, *Prohibition at its Worst* (New York: The Macmillan Co., 1926), 157.

5. Of course, not all industrialists favored Prohibition. Pierre S. duPont, chairman of the General Motors Corporation and E. I. duPont de Nemours Company, served as chairman of the Executive Committee of the Association Against the Prohibition Amendment.

These various concerns helped marshal a large coalition consisting of Protestant-based prohibition groups such as the Anti-Saloon League, the Women's Christian Temperance Union, industrialists, and intellectuals. They worked hard to get representatives elected who would vote for a Prohibition amendment. And they wanted an amendment to the Constitution, not just federal legislation. A law could be changed by a majority vote in Congress. With the growing importance of the urban population, it was only a matter of time before the urban influence over legislation would grow, proponents reasoned, so a Prohibition law could be easily abolished. A constitutional amendment was another thing. It would take a two-thirds majority in both houses of Congress and ratification by three-quarters of the states to change it. Thus, a minority of just thirteen state legislatures could block any effort to amend or abolish a Prohibition amendment.

The political activism by the prohibitionists paid off. By 1916, twenty-three states had adopted laws that closed the saloons and prohibited the manufacture of alcoholic beverages. The 1916 elections returned to Congress a supermajority favoring national Prohibition.

World War I also helped speed the progress of legislation. It did not go unnoticed that many U.S. breweries were owned by German Americans, and anti-German sentiments were running high. Congress adopted "temporary" wartime measures to conserve grain for the war effort. In September 1917, it banned the production (but not the sale) of distilled spirits until war's end. Also helping the Prohibition movement was the 16th Amendment, which established the income tax. The income tax greatly reduced the importance of the excise tax on alcohol as a revenue source for the government.

In December 1917, Congress approved the Prohibition amendment in a strong bipartisan vote (65–20 in the Senate and 282–128 in the House) and sent it to the states. The amendment prohibited the manufacture and sale of all alcoholic beverages, effective July 1919, again using wartime powers as an excuse. No saloon could operate legally after that date. By January 1919, the states had fully ratified the 18th Amendment, and it became the law of the land one year later in January 1920. Prohibition had actually begun in July 1919.

The National Prohibition Act, usually called the Volstead Act, was passed in 1919, over the veto of President Woodrow Wilson. It provided the legal framework for implementing the Prohibition amendment. The act prohibited "intoxicating liquors" (anything with alcohol content in excess of 0.5 percent) but made exceptions for alcohol sold for medicinal, sacramental, and industrial purposes. It also exempted "nonintoxicating" concentrated fruit or grape beverages made for personal use in the home, up to 200 gallons a year. All of these exceptions eventually helped topple Prohibition.

Why Did It End?

As early as 1928, very influential voices—such as Al Smith, the Democratic presidential candidate, a majority of the members of the American Bar Association, and wealthy individuals such as Pierre S. du Pont II—were calling for the repeal of Prohibition. By the late 1920s, if not much sooner, it was clear that Prohibition not only was a failure but also was creating severe problems for the country. In 1930 a group of respected, influential, and well-informed people were polled as to what they saw to be the major problems confronting the United States. Their responses produced the following ranking: (1) administration of justice, (2) Prohibition, (3) lawlessness and disrespect for law, (4) crime, (5) law enforcement, and (6) world peace. Unemployment was ranked 18th! The items ranked first, third, fourth, and fifth had become major concerns primarily as a consequence of Prohibition. When the poll was repeated in 1931, Prohibition was ranked as the most pressing problem, followed by administration of justice, lawlessness, and unemployment. So even with unemployment reaching 16.1 percent in 1931, Prohibition and Prohibition-related concerns still occupied the top three spots in the poll.[6] Democrats and Catholics led the charge against Prohibition, and in 1932, with the economy in depression, Democrats captured the White House.

Prohibition finally ended in 1933 with adoption of the 21st Amendment, passed by Congress in February 1933 and ratified by three-quarters of the states by December 1933. The 21st Amendment repealed the 18th Amendment, the only amendment ever to be repealed. The states ratified the 18th Amendment in record time of 13 months, but they set a new record in abandoning it in only 10 months. By 1936, all but eight states had changed their own laws making them at least partially "wet." Notably, some states never passed laws supporting

---

6. Frederick Lewis Allen, *Since Yesterday: the Nineteen-Thirties in America, September 3, 1929–September 3, 1939* (New York: Harper, 1940), 31.

Figure 1.2 A Democratic party poster promising happier days ahead.
Photo by The 1920s. 2004. Schaffer Library of Drug Policy. 17 Apr. 2004.
http://www.druglibrary.org/schaffer/history/e1930/prohibitionposter2.htm

Prohibition. The speed with which all this occurred helps illustrate how un-popular Prohibition had become.

The 21st Amendment was sent to the states with a novel requirement that states had to call a special convention of delegates elected by voters. This per-mitted a bypass of the many state legislatures that were still dominated by rural interests. After all, it would take only thirteen states voting no to stop the amend-ment.[7] The delegates were elected on the basis of their stand on the amendment. Prohibition came crashing down in a landslide: nationally 73 percent of the voters favored repealing Prohibition.

Prohibition ended because many original supporters, including elected of-ficials, came to realize two things. First, they had vastly underestimated the difficulties of preventing tens of millions of people from engaging in mutually beneficial exchanges: the buying and selling of alcoholic beverages. Essentially,

---

7. The Oregon experience illustrates the need to bypass the legislature. In both 1925 and 1931, the Oregon legislature refused to hold a referendum giving voters an opportunity to vote for or against repeal of Oregon's Prohibition law. Supporters of repeal finally used Oregon's initiative process to get the issue before the voters in November 1932; the vote was 206,619 in favor of repeal and 138,775 against. This ended state efforts to enforce Prohibition, although federal agents could still attempt to enforce the federal law. Source: Oregon state archives located at http://arcweb.sos.state.or.us/pages/exhibits/50th/prohibition1/repeal.html.

they had ignored a basic economic principle: if demand for an item—even an illegal item—is sufficient to make supplying it profitable, then entrepreneurs will always find ways to supply it. Second, they had failed to take into account properly the number and magnitude of adverse consequences created by Prohibition, including changes in consumer and producer behavior and undesirable impacts on government itself.

Consumer Behavior

Just as there presently is widespread disregard for speed limit laws, there was widespread disregard for Prohibition. In 1931 the National Commission on Law Observance and Enforcement (created by President Herbert Hoover to investigate enforcement of the Prohibition laws; hereafter, referred to as the Wickersham Commission, after its chairperson) concluded: "It is evident that . . . people of wealth, business men and professional men and their families, and perhaps the higher paid working man and their families are drinking in large numbers in quite frank disregard of the declared policy of the National Prohibition Act." The committee also found that there was much drinking among women and young people.

Drinking at homes, clubs, hotels, public dinners, and conventions was widespread. Tourists drank openly at summer and winter resorts. Drinking parties were hosted and attended by people of high standing and respectability. The Wickersham Commission found that after a brief period in the first years of Prohibition, there was a steady increase in drinking. In fact, historical trends suggest that per capita consumption likely would have surpassed pre-Prohibition levels by the mid-1930s, had Prohibition not been repealed.

Millions of people made their own home brews of wine, beer, or bathtub gin. Wineries sold concentrated grape juice along with the yeast that would cause the juice to ferment into wine. Due to an anomaly in the Prohibition Act, home manufacture of wine for personal consumption was effectively legal. The act stipulated that the wine should be "non-intoxicating," but in this connection, it did not define non-intoxicating. Thus, it became a question of fact to be determined by a jury from case to case. This obstacle effectively removed home winemaking from the purview of the Prohibition Act because it would have been too costly to enforce on a case-by-case basis. As a result, much homemade wine was produced, and a large amount of it found its way into circulation through black markets.

Many industrialists supported Prohibition for their employees, while continuing to drink themselves. Moreover, enforcement agents found it much easier to shut down a working person's "speakeasy" than to close up a large hotel where liquor flowed freely to influential and wealthy people. Furthermore, the wealthy were able to procure pure liquors, while the lower classes often had to contend with liquor of uncertain quality, risking poisoning from some impurity. All of these factors created the appearance that Prohibition exempted the wealthy while targeting the working classes, further turning public opinion against Prohibition.

Home distilling, while illegal, was nevertheless widespread. The commission noted that few things are more easily made than alcohol. While bathtub gin was usually of poor quality, it was cheap and effective, and its manufacture in the home was impossible to prevent. Thousands of small-scale breweries operated in people's basements. They were made possible by the development of "wort" or cooled boiled mash. This product contained no alcohol, so it was beyond the reach of the Prohibition laws. Yet, mixing wort with yeast produced beer, so small-scale brewing became simple, easy, and profitable for those choosing to sell some of their home production.

Prohibition did lead to significant increases in black-market liquor prices. In the mid-1920s beer prices were 700 percent greater than their pre-Prohibition levels; brandies cost about 400 percent more; and prices for spirits rose about 300 percent.[8] This change in relative prices caused many consumers to switch from beer (the most popular pre-Prohibition alcoholic beverage) to distilled spirits. As a percentage of total alcohol sales, spending on distilled spirits jumped from about 40 percent pre-Prohibition to 90 percent in 1922, and it remained above 70 percent until the repeal of Prohibition. So Prohibition had the unintended effect of causing millions of drinkers to switch to more potent alcoholic beverages.

The price increases actually caused total spending on alcoholic beverages to increase during Prohibition, even though per capita consumption fell. Price increases for alcoholic beverages also caused some people to switch to substi-

---

8. All of the data in this paragraph come from Mark Thornton, "Alcohol Prohibition Was a Failure," Cato Institute Policy Analysis No. 157, July 17, 1991.

tutes such as marijuana, cocaine, opium, and patent medicines.[9] Most of these products posed their own health hazards for users.

Supplier Behavior

Huge profits could be gained from illegally supplying alcoholic beverages: smuggling liquor, diverting industrial and medicinal alcohol, illicitly distilling and brewing, and "bootlegging," the illegal smuggling of alcohol.[10] The huge profits provided a basis for the growth in organized crime and made lavish bribery expenditures possible. Everyone engaged in the enforcement of the Prohibition law faced great financial temptations.

Smuggling of liquor was relatively easy and enormously profitable. The Wickersham Commission stated that smuggling was so profitable that smugglers had to land only one boat out of five in order to make a profit. The United States has about 15,000 miles of water borders and 3,700 miles of land borders. As late as 1925, only 280 federal agents were assigned to prevent smuggling by land across the Canadian or Mexican borders. The commission noted that a serious effort to prevent smuggling across those borders would require five to six times that number of agents.

The main source of smuggled liquor was Canada. One of the Radosevich brothers, according to family folklore, turned to smuggling Canadian whiskey. Liquor also came in from Mexico, Central America, the Bahamas, British Honduras, the West Indies, a group of French-owned islands off Newfoundland, and directly from Europe.

Preventing smuggling by land proved ineffective. To prevent smuggling by rail would have required unacceptable delays of legitimate freight. Moreover, any serious effort to curtail smuggling by rail required the assistance of the railroad companies, and they were not always cooperative with Prohibition

9. Good evidence of the extent of switching away from alcohol to illegal drugs isn't available. Boyan and Kleiman note that alcohol and marijuana are both mild depressants and are likely to be viewed as substitutes by consumers. David Boyum and Mark Kleiman, 2002, "Substance Abuse Policy from a Crime Control Perspective," in *Crime: Public Policies for Crime Control*, ed. James Q. Wilson and Joan Petersilia (Oakland, CA: ICS Press), 331–82.

10. Small-scale violators of the law often carried a flask of alcohol in their boot, and the term *bootlegging* gained acceptance as a term to describe all types of illegal trafficking.

agents. Smuggling by motor vehicle was similarly impossible to stop. The customs facilities at the major points of entry into the United States from Canada or Mexico were so crowded that thorough search and seizure efforts would have slowed border traffic to a crawl. Furthermore, adequate supervision of secondary roads and trails crossing our land borders was not practicable.

Smuggling by water created similar problems for customs and Coast Guard officials. Complete searches of ship cargoes would again unduly delay legitimate freight. The usual procedure was to examine 10 percent of the cargo, supposedly selected at random. However, dockworkers were easily bribed to avoid illicit liquor when selecting cargo for examination.

When enforcement efforts targeted a particular smuggling route or method, the smugglers easily shifted their transit chain. If a smuggling ring was broken up, another quickly replaced it. A top federal enforcement official estimated that in 1925 only about 5 percent of all smuggled liquor was intercepted by enforcement agents.[11]

The Prohibition Act unintentionally led to discovery of new and improved apparatus, new methods, and new materials for illicit production domestically. An especially important discovery was a new method of speedy aging, allowing for the production of good quality liquor in a very short time. The unlawful distilleries were so profitable that they had to operate only a short period to pay for themselves. When destroyed, they were easily replaced. The Wickersham Commission found that regardless of the number of seizures by enforcement agents, the total number of illegal distilleries in operation at the end of any period was at least as large as the number in existence at the beginning of that period.

The commission found a similar pattern with respect to retail establishments selling liquor, called speakeasies. Enforcement agents closed large numbers of them each year. Yet the total number in existence did not decrease as a result. As fast as they were closed, new ones sprang up. In most cities during Prohibition, the number of speakeasies greatly exceeded the number of pre-Prohibition saloons.[12] Estimates placed the number of speakeasies in Chicago at 10,000 in the late 1920s.[13]

---

11. Frederick Lewis Allen, *Only Yesterday: An Informal History of the 1920's* (New York: Harper and Row Publishers, 1931), 252.

12. Thornton, "Prohibition Was a Failure," 1991.

13. Allen, *Only Yesterday*, 265.

Illegal distilling was easy, commonplace, and highly profitable. Just as geography made smuggling relatively easy, it also made domestic production relatively safe and easy. Stills for the unlawful manufacture of spirits were easily hidden in uninhabited or sparsely inhabited areas near most cities. One of the Radosevich brothers turned to manufacturing spirits on an island on one of Minnesota's many lakes. A commercial still capable of producing one hundred gallons of liquor a day could be set up for as little as $500, about one-third the average worker's annual earnings. A one-gallon portable still could be had for about $6 or $7. It was simply impossible to prevent illegal distilling.[14] The enormous growth in the production of corn sugar, used primarily in illegal distilling, is revealing. Between 1919 and 1929 corn sugar production increased six fold. Overall, illicit distilling provided as much as 120 million gallons of whiskey and other spirits a year, around a gallon for every living American man, woman, and child.

Between nine and fifteen million gallons a year of legal industrial alcohol were diverted and sold for unlawful purpose.[15] Even though industrial alcohol contained additives—poisons required by the federal government that made it unsafe for human consumption—it was not difficult to extract the pure alcohol and then use it to make alcoholic beverages. Of course, unscrupulous types did not always extract the poison, so thousands died of alcohol poisoning during Prohibition. Humorist Will Rogers quipped: "Governments used to murder by the bullet only. Now it's by the quart."[16]

An interesting unintended consequence of Prohibition was that it led producers to substantially increase the alcohol content in their products. Stronger drinks meant reduced bulk, an important advantage when you are trying to keep your product hidden from enforcement agents. The potency of most alcoholic beverages rose 50 to 100 percent compared to the strength of such drinks either before or after Prohibition. Of course, this increased potency made the products more dangerous to consume. Alcohol poisoning was a serious problem during Prohibition.

Organized crime became the principal supplier of alcoholic beverages during this period. Thus, Prohibition played an important role in establishing the wealth and power of modern organized crime families. Al Capone's Chicago

---

14. Allen, *Only Yesterday*, 249.

15. Allen, *Only Yesterday*, 252.

16. Thornton, "Prohibition Was a Failure," 1991.

operation offers a good example. Federal authorities estimated that in 1927, Capone's illegal liquor operations were generating about $60 million in total revenue a year (in today's prices, that would be around $600 million a year).[17]

In addition to violating the Prohibition law, suppliers also committed other crimes, including murder, in their efforts to defend or expand sales territories, protect brand names, and enforce labor contracts. Again, Chicago provides a vivid example. In 1929 it was the scene of the infamous St. Valentine's Day massacre—memorialized in several movies and television programs—in which seven members of the O'Banion gang were lined up against a garage wall and shot in the back with machine guns because of an alcohol-related turf war. No one was ever arrested for this crime. During the 1920s and early 1930s, Chicago experienced more than 500 gang murders, most of them connected to Prohibition-related conflicts.[18]

As shown in Figure 1.3, the homicide rate in the United States jumped dramatically during Prohibition. In Prohibition's second year (1921), it soared 19 percent to 8.8 homicides per 100,000 people, the highest rate ever recorded in the United States up to that time. For the ten years prior to Prohibition, the homicide rate averaged 6.1 per 100,000 people; for the ten years after the end of Prohibition, it averaged 7.0. During the fourteen years of Prohibition, it averaged 8.4. The homicide rate in Prohibition's last year, 1933, was 9.7, a rate that the United States would not see again for four decades. While correlation does not prove causation, it is difficult to believe that the criminal activity surrounding Prohibition did not contribute greatly to this increase in homicides. Let's engage in a simple thought experiment. Suppose that in the absence of Prohibition, the homicide rate would have equaled 6.6, the average of the rates for the ten-year periods surrounding Prohibition. That implies that Prohibition resulted in an additional 29,000 homicides—roughly equal to the American lives lost in the Korean War![19] As a percentage of the U.S. population, that number far exceeds the number of U.S. deaths in the Korean War.

---

17. Allen, *Only Yesterday*, 264.

18. Allen, *Only Yesterday*, 263.

19. Emily Owens also finds evidence that the temperance movement raised homicide rates in the 20–30-year-old population. See Emily Owens, "The Birth of the Organized Crime? The American Temperance Movement and Market-Based Violence," *Department of Economics Seminar Series,* February 24, 2012, retrieved from http://economics.missouri.edu/seminars/files/2011/120224.pdf.

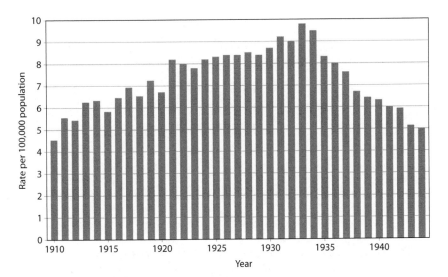

Source: U.S. Bureau of the Census, *Historical Statistics of the United States, Colonial Times to 1970* (Washington: Government Printing Office, 1975), part 1, p. 414.

Figure 1.3. Homicide rates: 1910–1944.

By 1930 public disregard for the Prohibition law was close to complete. Reports indicated that people were buying bootleg liquor in the halls of the U.S. Senate. In New York City, people patronized "cordial and beverage" shops that were openly selling alcoholic beverages; their only concession to the Prohibition authorities was that they did not display their wares in the shop windows. Furthermore, the well-heeled could take cruises beyond the twelve-mile limit for a weekend of boozing, the liquor obtained from ships anchored outside the reach of U.S. enforcement agents. People were making a mockery of Prohibition, especially in the cities.[20]

Government Behavior

One serious problem with Prohibition was that Congress and most state legislatures were unwilling to pay for more than token enforcement. Federal authorities had to rely mostly on state and local enforcement agents, and in many areas cooperation was minimal or nonexistent. Indeed, the Wickersham Commission found that a dozen or so states were still effectively "wet" as late as 1930.

20. Allen, *Since Yesterday*, 32.

Enforcement was supposed to be shared by federal, state, and local governments, according to the Volstead Act. Outright opposition to Prohibition in some states and cities, and lukewarm acceptance of it in others, represented a serious obstacle to effective enforcement of Prohibition in those places. Without cooperation from state and local authorities, federal agents had little success at enforcing the national Prohibition law. Interestingly, federal involvement in attempting to prohibit the production and sale of alcoholic beverages may have actually weakened overall enforcement efforts in states, where strong support for Prohibition had resulted in laws prior to adoption of the 18th Amendment. The commission noted that once the federal government got involved, many state officials saw enforcement of Prohibition as a federal concern and no longer a worry for them.

By 1923 state spending on Prohibition enforcement was about 13 percent of the amount they spent on enforcing their fish and game laws. Some states completely withdrew their contributions to Prohibition enforcement, thereby creating a virtually impossible enforcement problem for the federal agents.[21] Enforcement in the cities was made particularly difficult because of a general hostile attitude toward Prohibition. Many city dwellers saw Prohibition as an effort on the part of rural forces to mold city life into something that satisfied rural standards of conduct, and they resented it.

The commission concluded that without state cooperation, federal enforcement of the Prohibition act fails. They found that "as things stand now [in 1930], there is virtual local opposition [to enforcement]."[22] Illinois provides a good illustration. The state had stopped funding state enforcement efforts in the late 1920s. By 1930, the U.S. commissioner of prohibition reported that Prohibition enforcement in Illinois was bad in 27 counties, unsatisfactory in 16 more, very bad in Chicago, and bad in every other urban area of much importance.

Several states actually repealed their own prohibition laws during the 1920s and early 1930s. New York and Nevada repealed their statutes in 1923, and the people of Nevada voted to repeal the 18th Amendment in 1926. State prohibition laws were repealed by Montana in 1926, by Wisconsin in 1929, and by Massachu-

---

21. Allen, *Only Yesterday*, 251.

22. National Commission on Law Observance and Enforcement, "Report on the Enforcement of the Prohibition Laws of the United States," Schaffer Library of Drug Policy, 13, retrieved from http://www.druglibrary.org/schaffer/library/studies/wick/wick3.html.

setts, Illinois, and Rhode Island in 1930. Once off the state's books as a crime, incarceration of convicts would be at a federal facility and at federal expense.

In 1929, salaries for federal Prohibition agents were about $2,000 a year, compared with average annual earnings for full-time employees of $1,400. While they were not poorly paid relative to other workers, they were poorly paid relative to the bribes the criminal gangs could offer. Reportedly, Eliot Ness (known to many of us from the television series and the movie, both entitled *The Untouchables*) was offered $2,000 a *week* if he would leave Al Capone's illegal liquor operation alone. Ness refused the bribe, but many other enforcement agents apparently accepted them. The commission noted that it was common knowledge that large amounts of liquor were imported into the country or manufactured and sold, despite the law, with the connivance of agents of the law. More than two hundred federal prohibition agents were convicted on criminal charges, and hundreds of others were fired from their jobs for cause. Many of the agents were simply incompetent. Prohibition agents were not covered by civil service regulations until 1927. When they were finally required to take the civil service examination in order to keep their jobs, 59 percent of them failed. The federal Prohibition force also experienced low morale. Between 1920 and 1930, the annual turnover rate among the enforcement branch averaged an astonishing 40 percent. Not until 1927 was any effort made to furnish enforcement agents with any special training.

The strain on the court system was tremendous. By 1930 prosecutions in federal courts under the Prohibition Act were eight times the total number of all federal prosecutions in 1914. The workload was so overwhelming that prosecutors were forced to make bargains with defendants, allowing them to plead guilty to minor offenses and escape with light penalties. In 1930 nearly 90 percent of Prohibition convictions were of this sort. In some of the larger cities, where congestion in the federal court system was greatest, only about 5 percent of the convictions under the Prohibition Act resulted in some form of imprisonment. Small fines were the norm, at least in the larger cities. The criminal gangs, of course, viewed these fines as just another cost of doing business, easily covered by the enormous profits from supplying liquor.

The situation in state courts was no different, especially in urban areas where the Prohibition Act was generally resented. The case of St. Louis makes the point. In 1926, 96 percent of the fines imposed for Prohibition convictions were either "stayed" or substantially reduced to a trivial amount. Only 4 people out of 457 who pleaded guilty or were convicted at trial for a state Prohibition violation went to jail, with no term exceeding 60 days.

In the many areas where resentment against Prohibition was high, court authorities were forced to offer lenient deals to Prohibition violators. If the violators in these areas insisted on a jury trial, as they had a right to do, chances of conviction were slim as juries frequently refused to convict Prohibition violators.

Some people did go to prison. Al Capone, the notorious gangster bootlegger, did, but only for tax evasion. About 41 percent of all federal convictions under the Prohibition Act resulted in some form of imprisonment, straining the federal prison system. From 1914 to 1930, the number of federal convicts grew from around 4,000 to about 12,500. More than half of that growth was due to violations of the Prohibition Act, and some unknown but no doubt significant amount was due to crimes—like murder—stemming from activities related to Prohibition. In an effort to keep up with this surge in the prison population, federal spending on penal institutions increased 1,000 percent between 1915 and 1932. Nevertheless, severe overcrowding was the norm in most federal prisons. For example, Atlanta Penitentiary and Leavenworth Prison each had about 3,700 prisoners in 1929, far beyond their nominal capacity of 1,500 each.[23]

Finally, the effect of the Great Depression on tax revenues helped drive one more nail in Prohibition's coffin. Between 1873 and 1915, alcohol taxes provided between 50 percent and 80 percent of all internal federal tax revenues.[24] They were important only at the federal level during that period: local governments did not tax alcohol, while a few states raised a trivial amount of money by that means. Beginning in 1916, the federal taxes on personal and corporate income began to sharply reduce the relative importance of federal alcohol taxes. By 1919 alcohol taxes were raising only 9.4 percent of total federal revenues, even though the federal alcohol tax was generating record amounts of money. Income taxation allowed federal revenues to surge tenfold between 1916 and 1920. This mushrooming revenue stream undoubtedly encouraged some legislators

---

23. Thornton, "Prohibition Was a Failure," 1991.

24. During most of this period, customs duties provided half or more of all federal revenues. Alcohol taxes generated between 18 percent and 38 percent of total federal revenues over this period.

to vote in favor of Prohibition since the relative revenue loss from the alcohol tax would now be very modest.

However, income taxes are highly sensitive to business cycles. When the Great Depression hit, income tax revenues fell almost as much as the stock market. Between 1930 and 1933, individual income tax revenues plummeted 71 percent, and corporate tax revenues dropped 69 percent. The federal government needed money, and an alcohol tax was one way to get it. Of course, the government could not tax alcohol if its sale was illegal. It is probably no coincidence that Prohibition was abandoned in 1933. By 1935 the alcohol tax was the fourth most important source of internal revenue for the federal government: It raised almost as much as the federal tobacco tax, about 78 percent as much as the federal personal income tax, and about 71 percent as much as the corporate income tax.

Summing Up

Prohibition delivered on almost none of the promises made by its supporters. About all that can be claimed for Prohibition is that it temporarily lowered alcohol consumption in the early and mid-1920s. But much can be said on the negative side. Not only did Prohibition fail to alleviate the various ills as its supporters had claimed, it actually made most of them worse. It cost tens of thousands of jobs in the brewery and distilling industry, adding to recessionary forces in 1920 and 1921. It encumbered the public with startling new burdens to pay for enforcement and jails to hold those convicted, while simultaneously eliminating an important source of tax revenue; it corrupted politics, public servants, and public morals and lowered public respect for the law; it undermined the liberties and institutions on which the nation was founded; it promoted the killing, wounding, and poisoning of thousands; it created and enriched a criminal class who committed crimes on a grand scale. It is difficult, but not impossible, to imagine a more disastrous social policy.

The lesson here is that governmental efforts to prohibit adults from engaging in mutually beneficial exchanges are destined for failure and almost surely will produce a wide array of unintended and undesirable consequences. For example, laws against prostitution have never eliminated that activity. At the same time, they have helped to enrich criminals, who in turn can afford to bribe public officials; to spread venereal diseases including AIDS; to increase the crime rate; to place females in dangerous, often life-threatening situations; and to force females to depend on unsavory and often violent men for protection.[25]

A similar story can be told with respect to our forty-year War on Drugs. In fact, this chapter might have easily been devoted to the War on Drugs, which is nothing more than Prohibition revisited. After spending hundreds of billions of dollars[26] and imprisoning hundreds of thousands of people,[27] illegal drugs are still—and will continue to be—relatively cheap and widely available. The War on Drugs has had the same sort of unintended and undesirable consequences that Prohibition had. It has enriched a violent criminal class that will prey on this country for decades to come; it has hastened the spread of deadly diseases like AIDS and hepatitis; it has increased the crime rate; it has created an enormous tax burden, both to fight the war and to keep about a million people in prison; it has caused incredible violence, including drive-by shootings that often injure or kill innocent people; it has destabilized foreign governments; and it has created a general disrespect for the law. It is difficult to respect drug laws when President Bill Clinton, Vice President Al Gore, President George W. Bush, and President Barack Obama (among many other high profile individuals) are admitted, or quasi-admitted, one-time users of illegal drugs.

The War on Drugs is a failure for exactly the same reason the War on Booze was a failure. Government officials cannot stop people from engaging in mutually beneficial exchanges; they may reduce the extent of such exchanges with harsh penalties, but they won't stop them. Moreover, efforts to stop such exchanges will spawn many unintended and undesirable outcomes.

---

25. Probably the most common victims of serial killers are prostitutes.

26. Recently, two economists, Jeffrey Miron and Katherine Waldock, estimated that the War on Drugs is costing governments at all levels around $88 billion annually: $41 billion in law enforcement outlays and $47 billion in forgone tax revenues. Of course, the cumulative amounts over forty-some years are massive, probably exceeding $2 trillion since 1970 (in today's prices). Jeffrey Miron and Katherine Waldock, "The Budgetary Impact of Ending Drug Prohibition," Cato Institute, 2010.

27. About 500,000 people are now in local, state, and federal prisons on nonviolent drug-related offenses. http://www.nationalreview.com/corner/269208/prison-math-and-war-drugs-veronique-de-rugy.

A recent poll found that about 75 percent of U.S. adults think the War on Drugs is a failure. Why then does it continue? Several reasons come to mind. First, few taxpayers are probably aware of the explicit and implicit costs of the War on Drugs, about $88 billion a year or $380 per adult per year. The program is costing a family with two adults on average about $760 per year, a significant amount but perhaps not enough to get people to march in the streets to end the War, even if they were aware of the costs.

A second reason why a failed War on Drugs is likely to stretch into the distant future is that the dealers and users of the prohibited substances have little or no political clout (unlike the bootleggers, potential manufacturers, and customers for alcohol). If the War on Drugs routinely led to the arrest and imprisonment of higher income, politically connected Americans, it would have been abandoned, or at least scaled back, decades ago.

Portugal and Switzerland have taken much different approaches to drug usage. In 2001, Portugal became the first country to fully decriminalize personal drug usage; Switzerland emphasizes harm reduction, needle exchanges, and heroin-assisted therapy for addicts. Both countries have taken much of the profit out of drug dealing, and addiction rates have fallen. The United States might be better served to look to other countries for example.

The next chapter looks at the bungling of a government-created agency that turned a recession into the Great Depression.

2

Monetary Policy
During the Great Depression
How to Turn a Recession into a Depression

"Regarding the Great Depression. You're right, we [the Fed] did
it. We're very sorry. But thanks to you, we won't do it again."
—*Ben Bernanke*, chairman of the Federal Reserve System,
speaking at the Conference for the 90th birthday for
Milton Friedman, November 8, 2002

ON NOVEMBER 13, 1929, G. E. Cutler, the head of a prosper-
ous wholesale produce firm, entered the seventh-floor Wall Street law offices of
Fitch and Grant, seeking to speak to partner Grant Fox. Cutler grew increasingly agitated as he was told repeatedly that Fox was not available. Not being
able to take it any longer, Cutler opened one of the windows and scrambled
out onto the ledge. The following day, *The New York Times* reported the heroic
efforts of two other lawyers in the office to bring him back into the room. Their
valiant efforts failed. The distraught Mr. Cutler plunged to his death.

Mr. Cutler was reported to be a heavy loser in the October 1929 stock market
crash. His suicide was among the first that occurred during the darkest period of
U.S. economic history, known as the Great Depression. His plunge was symbolic
of the parallel plunges that were to continue for both the stock market and the
economy as a whole. Before the Great Depression ended, the U.S. suicide rate
reached a historical high, and nearly 25 percent of the labor force was thrown out
of work. Tragically, these dark days almost certainly could have been brightened
with the adoption of appropriate economic policies, especially monetary policies.
Ironically, the very institution that was created by Congress to prevent such a
catastrophic economic collapse, the Federal Reserve System, apparently caused
it, or at least greatly aggravated it.

Figure 2.1. Banking panics became commonplace during the Great Depression. Depositors congregate outside the state ordered closed doors of the Union Bank of New York City, 1931. Photo © Bettmann/CORBIS.

Banking Panics and the Need for a Central Bank

The Federal Reserve Act of 1913 was designed, as are most bills from Congress, to resolve a problem. The act created the Federal Reserve System, the Fed, the central bank for the United States. The Fed was expected to eliminate the frequent banking panics, or widespread runs on the banks, that had plagued our economy in previous years. A run on even a single bank is disruptive. If a run occurs on enough banks at the same time, the resulting chaos is a *banking panic*. Historically, banking panics trigger recessions, and recessions worsen banking panics. The Panic of 1907 is widely acknowledged as the key event that prompted Congress into speedy legislative action to create a U.S. central bank—although "speedy" evolved into six years.

To understand better the banking panics of this era, it is important to know that no federal deposit insurance existed and that banks, as always, made more promises than they could keep: They told depositors their money was safe and available for withdrawal. Checking accounts offer depositors the legal right to their money on demand (hence their formal name, demand deposits). Other accounts, such as savings accounts, may involve less instantaneous access to funds. However, banks usually kept far less than 100 percent cash backing, even for checking accounts.[1] A promise to give depositors their money on demand and not having cash in the bank or readily available from some other source can create problems. Under normal circumstances banks operated just fine without lots of cash in the vault. A run on the bank is a different story.

In the movie, *It's a Wonderful Life*, George Bailey's Building and Loan Association in Bedford Falls experiences a run. George, played by James Stewart, fends off the concerned depositors seeking their money with the plea that, while their money wasn't in the vault, it was safely invested nonetheless "in Joe's house . . . and a hundred others." George's impassioned speech saves the day, as depositors curb their enthusiasm for cash withdrawals; when the doors eventually close, only two dollars remain in the vault.[2] In reality, once a run began most banks went belly up. Anyway, you get the picture. When a run hits a bank, you've got trouble in River City and in Bedford Falls.

The Fed: Lender of Last Resort

The intent of the Federal Reserve Act of 1913 was to make banking panics a thing of the past. The Fed was to act as the bankers' bank. If a bank came under a run, the Fed was to advance cash sufficient to halt the run. It would loan the funds to the bank and take some of the bank's assets as collateral. The interest rate charged to the banks was dubbed the *discount rate*. The Fed's role was to serve as the lender of last resort. With sufficient cash readily available to meet any run on a bank, banking panics would be a thing of the past. At least that was the theory. Putting it into practice was another story. The biggest banking panic in U.S. history was in the making.

---

1. At the end of 1929, banks kept less than 11 percent in cash or deposits at the Fed as reserves backing demand deposits.

2. Formally, George's customers had savings accounts in which rights of withdrawal are not guaranteed on demand. Hence, George tells the customers that they are taking out loans, not making withdrawals.

The Great Depression

The period from the end of 1929 through 1933 was the darkest period of U.S. economic history. In 1929, the unemployment rate stood at 3.2 percent. By 1933, the unemployment rate had risen to 24.9 percent. Over this same period, inflation-adjusted national output declined 29 percent. Deflation occurred. The prices for goods fell 25 percent on average over the period, and the stock market did much worse, losing 80 percent of its dollar value. The hangover from the Great Depression was long lasting. Real national output did not recover to its 1929 level until 1937. Looking at it another way, during a stretch that lasted one-twelfth of the U.S. miracle economic century, there was zero real economic growth.

Experts on the Great Depression seem to agree that inappropriate Fed policy contributed substantially to the Great Depression. Some go further and claim that 1929 might have been the start of a mild recession if the Fed's mismanagement had not turned the situation into a disaster. Regardless, the evidence is clear that, despite the intentions of the Federal Reserve Act of 1913, the Fed failed to halt the worst banking panic in U.S. history. As a result, nine thousand banks, more than one-third of the number that existed in 1929, failed between 1929 and 1933. During the worst year, 1933, four thousand banks failed.

Throughout the Great Depression, runs on banks were commonplace, with substantial withdrawals occurring — in fact, the largest dollar amount of withdrawals as a percentage of bank deposits ever recorded. All told, the banking system lost 40 percent of its deposits, causing many of the bank failures. A modest dollar amount of bank withdrawals occurred in 1929, contributing to 659 bank failures. Withdrawals from banks intensified in 1930, and 1,350 banks failed. The year 1931 saw the worst run on banks during the Depression, as nearly 19 percent of bank deposits were withdrawn or simply lost—and 2,293 banks failed. In 1933, 4,000 banks failed, mostly because of high unemployment and the inability of borrowers to repay loans. Figure 2.2 puts these bank failures into historical perspective and provides evidence for the exceptionally large number of bank failures that occurred between 1930 and 1933. In 1933, the situation was so grave that a newly inaugurated president of the United States, Franklin D. Roosevelt, closed all banks for a "banking holiday."

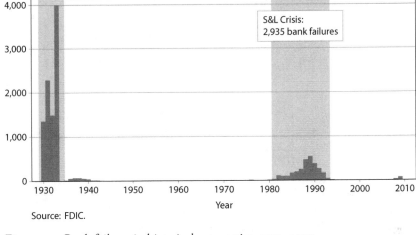

Source: FDIC.

Figure 2.2. Bank failures in historical perspective, 1930–2009.

At the same time that 40 percent of deposits were lost, bank lending plunged even more. Instead of making loans, banks put excess cash reserves into their vaults and bought U.S. Treasury securities that could easily be sold for cash, should another run occur.

The flight from deposits into cash is also seen in the public's preference for currency relative to checking deposits, using the currency-to-deposit ratio. In June 1929, the ratio was 0.16. This means that, on average, for every dollar in a checking account, the public held 16 cents in cash outside the banks. By June 1933, the ratio had risen to 0.33. For every dollar in a checking account, the public now held 33 cents in cash. This rise in the ratio was accomplished through bank withdrawals: Deposits fell dramatically as the public converted its deposits into cash, much of which was destined for hiding in residences.

The bottom line to all this is that massive amounts of cash were withdrawn from the banking system during the Great Depression. The loss of deposits meant that borrowers who had come to rely on banks as their source for loans now found that the well had run dry. Spending on goods and services plummeted. Bankruptcies soared. What triggered this? Why had the Fed failed so miserably in its mission to eliminate banking panics?

The Fed's Early Successful Years

At the beginning of the twentieth century, many Americans were concerned about concentrating power in Washington, preferring to keep power in the states, a sentiment still popular with states-rights advocates. The idea of a powerful central bank in the nation's capital met with considerable political resistance. So, in order to get congressional approval for the Fed, those who drafted the law made the Fed a decentralized institution with considerable independence from the federal government. Twelve regional Federal Reserve Banks were established. Each reserve bank had a board of directors, which appointed a governor.[3] These directors owed their appointments in large part to commercial banks in their districts who opted for membership in the Federal Reserve System and who voted for the directors of their regional Federal Reserve Bank. Each of the twelve Federal Reserve Banks was to engage in lending funds to banks within its region, as needed. Considerable decentralization of the Fed was achieved.

The Fed's early years were notable for its ability to achieve its objective of preventing banking panics. Heading the Fed in its earliest years was Benjamin Strong, governor of the New York Federal Reserve Bank.[4] Governor Strong was a knowledgeable and respected leader who ably led the fledgling Fed. Important to the Fed's success was the gradual discovery of a powerful new tool for altering bank reserves (cash in bank vaults and bank deposits at the Fed) and the amount of money in the banking system. The new tool was something called open-market operations.

Today, open-market operations are the primary means for affecting the amount of money and lending in the economy. Quite simply, open-market operations consist of Fed purchases or sales of government bonds. When the Fed wants to create money, it buys bonds by writing a check. Unlike you or me,

---

3. The twelve regional Fed-bank governors are now called *presidents* of their respective banks. The term *Governor* is now reserved for members of the Board of Governors. Seven governors make up the board (one of whom is designated the chairman, currently Ben Bernanke), headquartered in Washington D.C. Today, the regional presidents and governors combine to form the Federal Open Market Committee, the decision-making body for open-market operations.

4. Strong was governor of the Federal Reserve Board. The head of the Fed is now called the chairman.

the Fed does not need to worry about bouncing a check. When the Fed writes a check, it is the equivalent of printing new money. When the check enters the banking system, it eventually gets sent back to the Fed for cashing or for depositing by the bank at the Fed for future use. The Fed has more than enough paper money in its own vaults to ensure its ability to give the banks cash on demand.[5] When the Fed buys U.S. government bonds, it "monetizes the debt," creating money in exchange for the bonds. An open-market sale by the Fed does the reverse. When the Fed sells government bonds, it sells them from its previously purchased inventory and pulls the money from the sale out of the economy.

Open-market purchases give the Fed a second tool to fight banking panics. If the banking system is beset by withdrawals and banks are short on cash reserves, the Fed can simply write checks to buy bonds. When these checks get deposited into the banking system, banks send the checks to the Fed, creating new reserves for banks at the Fed that can be converted to cash. Open-market purchases and the direct lending of funds to banks at the "discount window" gave the Fed two powerful tools to combat banking panics, two ways to pump cash into the banking system. From its creation until Benjamin Strong's departure from the Fed in 1928, banking panics were nonexistent. Evidence of the Fed's success in raising confidence comes during the 1920s, as banks held few reserves in excess of those required by law. Banks were becoming convinced that banking panics were a thing of the past. Ironically, the Fed's initial success made the banking system even more vulnerable to the panic to come.

Fed Policy Failure During the Depression

The year 1929 started out well: strong real output growth, declining unemployment, no inflation, and a booming stock market. The stock market boom may have been too much of a good thing. Between June 1928 and June 1929, the stock market soared 31 percent. The stock market bubble was about to pop. When that happened in October 1929, it shook consumer and business confidence and started the economy on a downward path. The recession strained the ability of

---

5. The Fed gets this cash by asking the Bureau of Engraving and Printing to make it and pays them for their printing costs.

borrowers to repay loans to banks, which, in turn, shook depositor confidence. Banking panics started again.

Various explanations have been offered for the Fed's failure to halt the banking panics. These include ineptitude, sinister selfish motives, and the Fed's relative impotence in light of such a catastrophic economic collapse. Because the Fed is not a single entity but rather a conglomeration of individuals, there is plenty of room for all of these factors to have played roles.

Economists Milton Friedman and Anna Schwartz have argued that the departure of Chairman Benjamin Strong in 1928 is pivotal in explaining the subsequent policy failures of the Fed. Strong's successor, George L. Harrison, a lawyer and protégé of Strong, apparently lacked the respect and command authority of his predecessor. Some Fed governors had worried about the growing influence of the New York Fed, from which both Strong and Harrison hailed, and the use of the new policy tool, open-market operations, which diminished the role of the regional Federal Reserve Banks lending operations at their discount windows.

In March 1930, at the onset of the recession that eventually became the Depression, the Open Market Policy Conference,[6] the Fed committee in charge of all open-market operations, was expanded from five governors to include all twelve regional Fed presidents. This expansion shifted the balance of power within the Fed back to the regional Federal Reserve Banks. Harrison now found himself heading a substantially larger committee, one with many members intent on further strengthening the power of regional Federal Reserve Banks to fight banking panics. Harrison's ability to do the right thing with open-market operations was now greatly constrained.

Many of the Federal Reserve's governors were not particularly knowledgeable about economics and the connection between banking and spending in the economy. When panics occurred and banks began failing, some governors voiced the opinion that the bank failures indicated bank management problems and were of no concern to the Fed. It was not widely understood that a banking panic threatened even the most secure bank, if quick liquidation of assets to meet withdrawals required "fire sale" pricing of those assets. Economic losses on the fast sale of assets could quickly erode a bank's net worth and lead to bank-

---

6. This committee is now called the Federal Open Market Committee.

ruptcy. Other governors pointed to the low discount rate set by the Fed once the Depression began as evidence of an already active antirecessionary monetary policy. Given the deflation during this period, no one seemed to notice that real (inflation adjusted) borrowing costs to the banks were actually very high.

The Fed's discount rate, its lending rate to banks, hit a low of 1.5 percent in mid-1931. The inflation rate in 1931 was a negative 8.8 percent. That is, the average price of goods and services declined by nearly 9 percent. The real cost of borrowing from the Fed exceeded 10 percent. The principal and interest that a bank needed to repay the Fed after a one-year loan could buy 10 percent more real goods. The following numerical example may help to illustrate this. Assume you receive a $1,000 loan from a rich aunt to take a cruise. Your aunt helps you out by giving you the loan interest free. Assume prices fall 50 percent over the year, a 50 percent deflation rate. You repay the $1,000 after one year. You are now repaying the equivalent of two cruises. Your real borrowing cost was extremely high—you borrowed the equivalent of one cruise and repaid the equivalent of two cruises—even though auntie gave you the loan for "free."

A sinister motive for permitting the banking panic to run its course comes from identifying the types of banks that failed most frequently: small country banks with state charters that did not belong to the Federal Reserve System. The Fed member banks, especially the most influential members, were big-city banks. These big banks stood to gain market share by entering into the collapsed banking markets, if state law permitted branch banking or bank holding companies. It seems cynical to suggest a motivation that might have encouraged bank failures, but indeed, some influential banks affiliated with the Federal Reserve benefitted from the banking panics and bank failures during the Great Depression.

In the Fed's defense, a case can be made that the legislative powers given to the Fed, along with existing banking laws, made the Fed's task of preventing bank failures during the Great Depression difficult. No bank deposits were federally insured during the Depression. Had the Federal Deposit Insurance Corporation (FDIC) existed as a complement to the Fed, banking panics almost assuredly would have been avoided. In 1934, the creation of the FDIC produced a great calm in banking; the number of bank failures plummeted to a mere 57 from 4,000 in the previous year. Thus, inadequate institutional arrangements during the Depression put the Fed in a difficult position.

The Fed may have also felt that it was constrained from aggressively dealing with the bank panic. Discount loans could be made only if the bank had certain "eligible paper" for collateral. Most banks' financial assets (most of their loans, for example) did not count as eligible paper. The Fed may have also been concerned about stepping beyond the bounds of the requirements set by the gold standard. At the time of the Great Depression, U.S. money was backed by (at least to a certain percentage) and convertible into gold. The printing of paper money by the Fed without proper gold backing or without increases in gold holdings by the Fed was perceived as being risky or even illegal.

The Lesson

Today, most economists are convinced that another Great Depression can be avoided, or at least that the Fed will not contribute to turning a recession into a depression. Vastly improved understanding of monetary policy and expanded lending powers of the Fed make such a dramatic collapse of bank lending and another depression unlikely. The recession of 2007 to 2010 provides a good example.

That recession had the potential to be even worse than the Great Depression. The burst of the real-estate bubble, along with the stock market collapse, triggered a substantial shock to Americans' wealth: the loss was greater than the one caused by the collapse in stock prices in 1929. If the Fed's response to the recent recession had been the same as its response during the Great Depression, the dollar amount of bank deposits would have declined by nearly fifty percent. Bank lending would have collapsed by far more than it did, and unemployment would have soared even higher. The Fed was able to keep bank deposits growing by engaging aggressively in open-market purchases that pumped money into the banking system.[7] Milton Friedman noted that Fed inaction during the Great Depression turned a recession into the Depression. Fed action in 2007 to 2010 kept the Great Recession from becoming another Depression. Figures 2.3 and 2.4 depict the Fed's contrasting management of the money supply during the Great Depression and the recent recession.

---

7. Interestingly, many of the open-market purchases involved mortgage-backed securities rather than U.S. Treasury bonds.

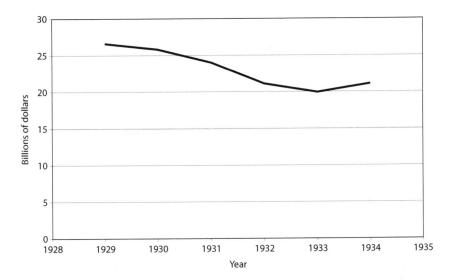

Source: Historical Statistics of the United States: Colonial Times to 1970
(Washington: Department of Commerce, Bureau of the Census. 1975).

Figure 2.3. Money supply (M1) during Great Depression in billions of dollars.

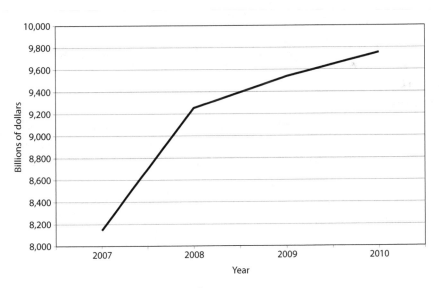

Source: St. Louis Federal Reserve Bank.

Figure 2.4. Money supply (MZM) during recent recession in billions of dollars.

Between 1929 and 1933, the money supply, made up primarily of bank deposits, declined by about 25 percent. In contrast, from the end of 2007 to the end of 2010, the money supply *grew* nearly 20 percent. The Fed's actions to prevent the money supply from falling in the recent period helped keep the economy from Great Depression II. While Fed decision makers now understand much more about monetary economics than they did in the 1930s, Fed's policy decisions remain discretionary, the product of individual decision-making, not the product of rules. Discretionary policy carries with it the risk that considerably less efficacious individuals may someday take control of the Fed. Should such a risk be a concern? History suggests it should be.

In 1978, industrialist G. William Miller was President Jimmy Carter's surprise nomination for chairman of the Fed. Chairman Miller held degrees in marine engineering and law and had risen to become the head of Textron, Inc. With inflation seemingly out of control, Miller was to take the reins of the single-most important organization able to fight the inflation. The Senate's Banking Committee Chairman William Proxmire told his colleagues that Mr. Miller was unqualified by training, education, or experience to become the nation's top banker. Supporters of Miller called him "a strong leader in the business fraternity," "an intelligent, skillful businessman," and "a tonic for business confidence." After two hours of debate, the Senate overwhelmingly confirmed Miller. Supporters had made Miller plausibly acceptable. When he left the Fed, the inflation rate was 14 percent, considerably worse than when he arrived.

Since Miller's departure, monetary policy has had a better, if not perfect run. Some economists, the author included, think it would be better if the Fed operated by a rule rather than at the discretion of individuals. Milton Friedman was a long-time advocate of a money supply rule that would force the Fed to make a modest increase in the money supply every year. Another possible rule, one already imposed by a number of other central banks, would require the Fed to have one goal: overall price stability or a very low inflation rate. These rules would prevent the Fed from taking some discretionary actions that might prove useful in the short run; on the other hand, they would prevent the Fed from making some colossal inflationary or deflationary blunders. For example, the deflation and monetary blunders during the Great Depression would not have occurred, had the Fed been under a money supply or an inflation rule.

Another Fed blunder that could have been avoided if a rule had been in place is detailed in the Nixon-Burns political business cycle chapter.

Summing Up

If the Fed was in fact responsible for turning a recession into the Great Depression, its mishandling of monetary policy during this period makes it rank near or at the top of economic blunders of the past hundred years. How costly was the Fed's blunder? Let's engage in a thought experiment to get some estimate. Let's assume from 1931 through 1935 the U.S. economy had experienced a severe but more normal recession and that the unemployment rate during this period averaged 10 percent.[8] Let's also assume that any unemployment rate above this amount was due to the Fed's blundering. For these five years, the Fed would then be responsible for raising the unemployment rate by 5.9, 13.6, 14.9, 11.7, and 10.9 percentage points. We can translate these increases in the unemployment rate into losses of production and income for the economy using something called Okun's law. Using Okun's law, the average annual decrease in production and income caused by this increase in the unemployment rate is about 23 percent. To put this into perspective, if such an event occurred in the United States today, the total dollar loss of production and income over five years would be about $15.5 *trillion*. Of course, the actual amount could be more, as the bungled monetary policy during the Depression produced a hangover effect that lasted for the rest of the decade. Furthermore, the Fed's bungling produced other worldwide costs because the U.S. Depression contributed to triggering depression globally. On the other hand, using Okun's law for such large deviations from normal probably overstates the numbers, so the $15.5 trillion amount should be considered just a rough "guesstimate." Even if the actual amount is half as much, the Fed's mishandling of the Great Depression must be ranked as one of the biggest economic blunders of the past one hundred years.

The next chapter details another Depression-era blunder: the worst trade bill in U.S. history.

---

8. Starting the calculations in 1931 allows for some lag in the effect on the economy of the Fed's blundering.

3

The Hawley-Smoot Act

Holy Smoke, We Started a Trade War!

". . . the most destructive trade bill in history."
—*President Ronald Reagan*

"A tariff war does not furnish good soil for the growth of world peace."
—From a petition of American economists

IT WAS 1930, and the U.S. economy was well into recession. Unemployment was rising rapidly, and national output plunging. Congress, concerned with an impending election, sensed the need to take action to placate nervous voters. Its solution was the Hawley-Smoot Act, the brainchild of Republican Congressman Willis Chatman Hawley (Oregon) and Republican Senator Reed Smoot (Utah) (shown in Figure 3.1). The act was passed by a Republican-dominated Congress, yet it only squeaked through the Senate by two votes. The final act raised the tax on imported goods to their highest levels in more than one hundred years. The act raised tariffs on more than a thousand imported products.

Congressional debate was acrimonious, with widely divergent views on the desirability of the legislation. Senator James E. Watson (R-Indiana) claimed Hawley-Smoot would put the United States "on the up-grade financially, economically and commercially" within thirty days. In contrast, Senator Furnifold M. Simmons (D-North Carolina) said, "The most disastrous times this country has ever seen will befall this country as the result of this law." Industrialist Henry Ford weighed in, calling the act "an economic stupidity."

Figure 3.1. Willis C. Hawley (left) and Reed Smoot meeting shortly after the
signing of the Smoot-Hawley Tariff Act. Both men were soon to be
voted out of office. Photo by National Photo Company Collection
(Library of Congress).

More than a thousand U.S. economists signed a letter urging a rejection
of Hawley-Smoot and urging a veto from President Herbert Hoover, should
Congress pass it. The letter detailed the economic folly of the act and pointed
out other expected costs:

> Finally, we would urge our Government to consider the bitterness which
> a policy of higher tariffs would inevitably inject into our international
> relations. The United States was ably represented at the World Economic
> Conference, which was held under the auspices of the League of Nations
> in 1927. This conference adopted a resolution announcing that "the time
> has come to put an end to the increase in tariffs and move in the opposite
> direction." The higher duties proposed in our pending legislation violate
> the spirit of this agreement and plainly invite other nations to compete
> with us in raising further barriers to trade. A tariff war does not furnish
> good soil for the growth of world peace.[1]

---

1. *Congressional Record-Senate*, of May 5, 1930, 8327–30.

The letter was read into the Congressional Record on May 5, 1930. It did no good. The House and Senate Conference Committee passed a unified bill on June 13, and President Hoover signed the bill into law on June 17.

Ironically, more than fifty years after its passage, Republican President Ronald Reagan referred to the Republican-sponsored Hawley-Smoot Act as "the most destructive trade bill in history." While the exact magnitude of the act's impact on the economy still is debated today, economists widely agree that the act quite predictably yielded considerably more costs than benefits, contributed to intensifying the Great Depression, and helped set the stage for World War II. The act and the story of its passage also highlight Congress at its worst in pandering to special interests. All told, the Hawley-Smoot Act is a worthy member of the worst economic policies of the past hundred years.

The Case for Free Trade

While many jokes exist about the inability of economists to reach agreement, economists come close to unanimity in their support for free trade.[2] As the textbooks explain, free trade promotes economic efficiency and competition and allows every nation to be a net winner. However, not every individual or firm within a country gains from free trade, and this fact of economic life is the primary reason free trade remains an unobtainable goal.

Consumers clearly benefit from buying foreign goods. Otherwise, why would they buy them? But domestic producers competing against the imports lose when consumers buy foreign goods and domestic production and sales decline as a result. When competing with imports, the prices for domestically produced goods must fall to maintain sales. Economists estimate that the gains to consumers exceed the losses to domestic producers, with a positive net gain. In other words, gainers gain more than losers lose, but this is little solace for the losers.

When domestically produced goods are exported, there are also winners and losers, but the tables are turned. Domestic producers gain from exporting because they receive a higher price overseas than they would get in an exclusively

---

2. A 2005 survey found that 87.5 percent of economists surveyed agreed that the "the U.S. should eliminate remaining tariffs and other barriers to trade." Robert Whaples, "Do Economists Agree on Anything? Yes!" *The Economists' Voice*, 3, Issue 9 (2005), Article 1.

domestic market. The domestic price must rise to match what the foreigners are paying, and this hurts domestic consumers. But once again, in weighing the costs and benefits, economists conclude that benefits exceed costs. In this case, domestic producers gain more than domestic consumers lose.

Summing up, both the import and the export of goods and services produce net gains to society. This fact leads almost all economists to support free trade between nations. While free trade provides net benefits, the distribution of benefits certainly is not uniform. Some people lose, and some countries gain more than other countries. Since each country's economic pie is bigger after trading, economists generally favor free trade and try to devise ways to soften the blow to the losers.

This is the "static" reason to support international trade, and it also helps to generate a more favorable "dynamic" situation as well. Over time, the increased competition caused by international trade yields better products—more efficient voltaic cells and swifter laptops—than would have resulted in the absence of international trade. Finally, some economists also support free international trade on civil libertarian grounds. Why should the government control or restrict transactions of legal goods between consenting individuals?

The Case for Restricting International Trade

Losers from international trade have a strong incentive to reverse their plight by lobbying the government for "protection." Industries that lose customers to foreign producers can be expected to make an impassioned plea to their government to protect them from the foreign invasion. Protection can come in many forms: quotas that restrict the quantity of a foreign good allowed into a country, tariffs that impose a tax on imported goods at the border, quality standards that (only coincidentally!) match exactly the quality of the domestically produced goods, voluntary export restraints that convince the foreign producers to "voluntarily" curb their exports, or, in the extreme, a complete prohibition on the importation of a foreign-produced good or service.

Exporting industries also get into the legislative process to make their gains even larger. Industries seek export subsidies to make their products more attractive to foreigners. Examples include low-interest loans made by the U.S. Export-Import Bank to foreigners who make large capital goods purchases in the United

States and European subsidies given to Airbus, whose output is largely exported. Not unexpectedly, the large group of unorganized consumers have little voice when governments consider protectionist legislation or export subsidies.

All import-restricting policies raise the prices of the protected goods. To grease the bad-policy machine, supporters of protectionist policies must find plausibly acceptable reasons for the trade interference. There are quite a few.

One of the most popular arguments in support of trade protection is the *cheap foreign labor* argument. Domestic producers may claim that they suffer unfairly because foreign workers earn so little, or perhaps work under "inhumane" conditions. Economists don't find this argument terribly compelling; low wages are usually the result of low productivity. If trade provides a society with net benefits, eliminating or reducing trade must produce net losses to society. The economists' benefit-cost criteria indicate that protection, in the overwhelming majority of cases, is economically undesirable.

Another popular argument for protection is the *infant industry* argument. Supporters argue that an industry would be competitive internationally if only it could receive some protection (subsidy) until it matured. While this may prove true in some special cases, economists point to the more likely outcome: The industry will require protection after it matures and even up until the moment of its death. Infant industries rarely grow up to the point where they can stand independently, and so subsidies to industries have a habit of lingering. As a general rule, expected costs exceed expected benefits when protecting infant industries.

Some industries argue that they are crucial to national defense in the event of war, when foreign supplies may become undependable. Thus, protection of these industries may be necessary to ensure stable and sufficient supplies of these essential goods. While this argument has merit in some special cases, nearly every industry thinks it is crucial to the economy in the event of war. The lace curtain industry offered one particularly creative explanation in its plea for protection. In the event of war in tropical areas, so the industry claimed, mosquito netting, a closely related product to lace curtains, would be essential. If national defense benefits from protecting an industry, these gains must outweigh the economic losses associated with protective barriers to pass the benefit-cost criteria.

One of the worst arguments for supporting protective barriers is the *beggar thy neighbor* argument. Increases in protective barriers, because they raise the price of foreign goods, can be expected to raise domestic demand. If tariffs can be raised on a sufficiently large number of items, the increase in spending on domestically produced goods is likely to boost total economic activity, perhaps even bumping an economy out of recession. The exporting country experiences a corresponding decline in sales. Thus, the economy that imposes widespread protective barriers is, to some extent, exporting its recession to foreign countries, reducing the economic well-being of their trading "neighbors."

The error of the beggar-thy-neighbor argument arises from an unrealistic assumption that the foreign nation or nations would do nothing in response to the trade actions adversely affecting them. More than likely, the foreign country would retaliate and touch off a "trade war." This brings us to the story of the Hawley-Smoot Act.

The Hawley-Smoot Act

Congress began discussion of what was to become the Hawley-Smoot Act in early 1929, months before the onset of the recession that became the Great Depression. The initial purpose of the legislation was to provide assistance to the hard-hit agricultural sector, which seriously lagged behind the manufacturing sector of the economy. Fortunately for the manufacturing sector, the debate in Congress dragged on for months. Agriculture got the camel's nose under the tent, and the manufacturing camel was soon to follow. The stock market crash in October 1929 and the economy-wide recession in 1930 brought U.S. industry to Washington, also pleading its case for protection. As so often happens when competing groups get involved in congressional legislation, the final act passed in June 1930 looked nothing like the legislation that was originally envisioned. In fact, the agricultural states that were originally the act's supporters and intended beneficiaries became its primary opponents as they realized that all the tariffs on manufacturing goods would make them net losers from the legislation. Farmers saw that the act would raise the prices for the things they bought more than it would raise the prices of the things they sold. A *New York Times* headline succinctly summed it up: "Industrial States Swing Tariff Vote, Aligned Against Farm West and South."

Industry wanted protection, and protection is what it got. The average tariff on protected goods was 53 percent. In today's terms, a $20,000 imported automobile would be hit with a $10,600 tax at the border. Consumers would see the price of their $20,000 imported automobile increase to $30,600. While the average tariff rate was 53%, there was considerable variation: wool and manufactures using wool, 59.83%; earth, earthenware, and glassware, 53.64%; sugar, molasses, and manufactures thereof, 77.21%; agricultural products and provisions, 34%; brooms, 25%; dolls, 90% (in plenty of time for Christmas).[3]

The Congressional Record reveals why the Hawley-Smoot Act took so long to reach a final vote. Nearly every item imaginable fell under the act, and tariffs needed to be "properly" set. As examples, cows weighing less than 700 pounds would be taxed at 24.4 cents per pound (this and subsequent prices have been converted into 2010 dollars), cows weighing more than 700 pounds would be taxed at 39 cents a pound, sweet clover seeds 52 cents per pound, red clover seeds $1.04 per pound, white clover seeds 79 cents per pound, ladino clover seeds 79 cents per pound, alsike clover seeds $1.04 cents per pound, other clover seeds 39 cents per pound. Other issues needed debate and possible amendments to the act. Cement was previously free from tariffs, but the new proposed tariff rate would add an estimated $520 million (2010 dollars) to the government's cost of new highway construction. However, after debate, an amendment that would have exempted public works projects from the cement tariff was eventually eliminated from the Act. Congressional debate also swirled around the parcel post regulations concerning the import of Cuban cigars (facing a 70% tariff rate). Should Congress require 300 cigars to the package or 3,000? These were difficult issues, no doubt. Eighteen months after the bill was first brought to Congress, the final votes were taken.

Congressman John Nance Garner (D-Texas) summed things up: "These hearings, ostensibly for the relief of agriculture, degenerated into an orgy of rate boosting for the industrial interests. Never in the history of American tariff making had that spectacle been equaled."[4] David S. Muzzy, then professor of history at Columbia University, estimated the cost of the protracted congressional debate at the time at $2 million ($26 million in 2010 dollars).[5] However, this was a pittance compared to the cost associated with the act's ultimate effects on trade and the economy.

---

3. Sources: Congressional Record-House, June 14, 1930, and *U.S. News and World Report*.

4. Source: Congressional Record-House, June 14, 1930, 10763.

5. Source: Congressional Record-House, June 14, 1930, 10764.

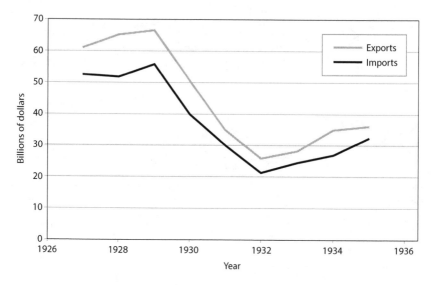

Source: Historical Statistical Abstract of the U.S., series U 249–263, p. 895; and author's calculations.

Figure 3.2. U.S. Imports and Exports, 1927–1935 (billions of 2010 dollars). Trade volume peaked in 1929. Hawley-Smoot Act passed in 1930.

Figure 3.2 shows U.S. imports and exports during the period from 1927 to 1935.[6] In 1929, U.S. imports totaled $55.7 billion (again, all numbers are 2010 dollars). In 1930, U.S. imports plunged to $39.9 billion due to intensifying recession and a half-year of Hawley-Smoot. In 1931, the first full year of the act, imports fell further, to $29.9 billion. Imports in 1931 were nearly half their value for 1929. Clearly, worsening U.S. economic conditions caused much of this reduction, but one economist estimates that the act may be responsible for about 25% of the reduction[7] or about $4 billion to $6.7 billion annually. Did this help to moderate the U.S. recession? Was the United States successful in beggaring its neighbors? The act failed miserably.

In 1929, exports stood at $66.4 billion. By 1931, exports had declined to $34.5 billion. Thus, exports declined by $31.9 billion while imports were declining by

---

6. Sources: Historical Statistical Abstract of the U.S., Series U 249–63 and author's calculations.

7. Source: Irwin, Douglas A. 1998. The Smoot-Hawley Tariff: A Quantitative Assessment. *The Review of Economics and Statistics* 80 (2) (May): 326–34.

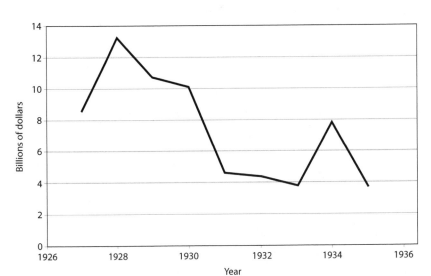

Source: Historical Statistical Abstract of the U.S. series U 249–263, p. 895; and author's calculations.

Figure 3.3. Net Exports (Exports less Imports), 1927–1935
(billions of 2010 dollars).

only $25.8 billion. Foreign retaliatory tariffs as well as foreign recessions worked to the disadvantage of the United States. The nation had triggered a tariff war, and the foreigners had won.

Net exports—exports minus imports—are shown in Figure 3.3. Net exports are commonly used by economists to measure the effect of foreign trade on aggregate spending in an economy. If net exports are positive, a country has a trade surplus, and trade adds positively to spending on domestic output; if net exports are negative, a country has a trade deficit, and trade reduces spending on domestic output. During the period from 1927 to 1930, net exports averaged about $10.7 billion (2010 dollars). During the period from 1931 to 1934, net exports fell to $5.2 billion—a reduction in our trade surplus of nearly 50 percent. Thus, the trade war started by the United States led to a substantial reduction in the U.S. trade surplus and a reduction in net spending on U.S. goods, exactly the opposite result intended by the supporters of Hawley-Smoot.[8] This helped push the U.S. economy further into recession.

---

8. In calculating the effect of Hawley-Smoot on net exports, it is assumed that worldwide recession caused equal effects on U.S. imports and exports.

Foreign retaliation was not unexpected. Actually, retaliation was under way while Congress plodded through its final debates on Hawley-Smoot. Prior to passage, it was reported that

> The Canadian Government has proclaimed about 500 tariff increases of its own and is putting them into effect, subject to later approval of Parliament... Products of American export are particularly singled out... Canada insists that its swing away from free trade is not an expression of its ill will towards America. It is viewed rather as a necessity that was dictated by the American tariff [Hawley-Smoot].[9]

Foreign governments publicly had promised tariff retaliation against the U.S. months before passage of Hawley-Smoot. Before the House's final vote, the *New York Times* reported: "Behind the storm of European resentment against the new American tariff schedule is a calm, calculated scheme for effective reprisals, which if carried to its logical conclusion, may cause the loss of hundreds of millions of dollars to the American export trade."[10]

Figure 3.4 shows the dramatic contraction in global international trade following passage of Hawley-Smoot in 1930. Between 1929 and 1933, world trade decreased by 67 percent. Much of this decrease came from global recessionary forces, and many countries would have likely imposed new tariffs to beggarthy-neighbors out of recession anyway, but the United States had the dubious distinction of firing the first shot in the world trade war.

Douglas Irwin, in *Peddling Protectionism,* points out a particularly damaging consequence of Hawley-Smoot.[11] The act and the ill will it generated gave rise to discriminatory trade policies and tariffs specifically aimed to hurt U.S. exports. Great Britain, for example, established a preferential tariff arrangement between it and its former colonies, much to the detriment of the United States. Switzerland, hurt badly by U.S. tariffs on watches, organized a successful informal boycott of U.S. goods. Eighty percent of Italy's imports of automobiles came from the United States, so doubling its tariff on automobiles particularly hurt the United States. Most countries were signatories to the Most Favored

---

9. Source: Editorial from the *St. Paul Pioneer Press,* entered into Congressional Record-Senate, June 13, 1930, 10615.

10. *New York Times,* June 14, 1930, 1.

11. Douglas A. Irwin, 2011, *Peddling Protectionism* (Princeton: Princeton University Press).

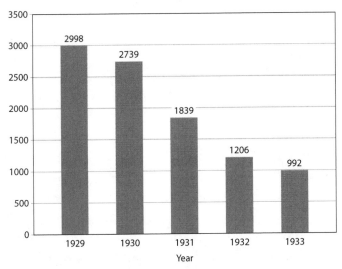

Plummeting World Trade

Source: Charles Kindleberger, *The World in Depression*, 1929–1939
(Berkeley: University of California Press, 1973).

Figure 3.4. Recession and tariffs combine to bring down international trade.

Nation agreement, which required that a country imposing a tariff on a good had to apply the tariff equally to all countries. But trade restrictions based on health and safety restrictions did not violate this agreement. Soon after passage of the act, Great Britain and Argentina found some U.S. apples and U.S. eggs to be unsanitary.

The question remains, why did Congress pass such a counterproductive law? A number of plausible answers exist. First, 1930 was an election year, and many in Congress must have felt that some action was needed to appease voters' concerns about recession. Some may have mistakenly felt Hawley-Smoot would help the economy. Regardless, the real consequences of the act might take years to determine; elections were immediate. Protecting U.S. jobs by raising tariffs was plausibly acceptable to workers. Once the tariff movement began, each industry was under pressure to receive at least average protection or lose ground. An industry eventually would be damned if it supported the act by lobbying for its interests, but more damned if it didn't. In contrast, agricultural interests figured that they did relatively poorly and bailed out in their support for the act. Adding to U.S. agriculture's concern was that many agricultural products were exported. The anticipated foreign tariff retaliation was expected to hit farm interests hard. In the end, states with important industrial interests garnered more votes than did the agricultural states.

The Hawley-Smoot Act and foreign retaliation likely worsened the U.S. recession by reducing net exports. The alleged intent of the act was to put the U.S. economy on the road to recovery. It failed miserably in creating jobs. Much more onerous to the economy were the economic losses from reducing trade and the subsequent loss of benefits that trade brings. Losers lost more than gainers gained. On yet another level, the act established a new way of doing business in Washington. U.S. special interest groups found that the increasing power of the federal government could be directed to garnering *legislative profits*, economic gains that arise from favorable legislation. This strategy may have backfired in the case of Hawley-Smoot, but the possibility of using federal legislation to improve profits helped to pave the way for the New Deal and for substantial growth in government spending and in regulatory activities. Much too often, these served special interests at the expense of the public interest.

Both Representative Hawley and Senator Smoot were defeated in their 1932 reelection bids, and the controversial and ineffective act that bore their names played some role, perhaps not a major one. President Franklin D. Roosevelt helped to roll back tariffs in 1934 with the Reciprocal Trade Agreements Act, but trade restrictions remained high and were not seriously reduced until the end of World War II.

Ongoing Trade Interventions and the Cost of Saving American Jobs

While tariff rates are substantially lower than in the days of Hawley-Smoot, trade barriers are by no means eliminated. Industries seeking protection have increasingly turned to import quotas, antidumping penalties, and other nontariff barriers. The net result is the same: higher prices for consumers. The 2002 Annual Report of the Federal Reserve Bank of Dallas put price tags on protecting various jobs in the United States.[12] The total cost to consumers for protecting

---

12. "The Fruits of Free Trade," 2002 Annual Report of the Federal Reserve Bank of Dal-

jobs was estimated to be nearly $100 billion annually. This number is computed by multiplying the *increase* in the price of the protected good with the amount of the good that consumers buy—indicating how much *more* consumers must pay for the protected items. But the trade protection raises output in these protected industries and leads to more employment. Is it worth it? The average cost to consumers for a job saved was more than $231,000. The employment effects aren't very large relative to the increased costs to consumers. It costs consumers more than $1 million to save one job in either the benzoid chemical or the luggage industry. Using trade protection to save jobs ain't cheap!

Restricting imports remains a popular vote-getting activity for presidents. President Ronald Reagan, for example, wanted to help out the U.S. autoworkers but struggled with violating his "free trade" philosophy. His vice president, George H. W. Bush, came up with a new and especially creative solution: voluntary export restraints (VERs). The Japanese were told that, given the mood in Congress, tariffs on their autos were inevitable, unless they voluntarily limited shipments to the United States. The Japanese complied, the reduced supply of autos raised their prices, U.S. production of autos increased, and free-trade principles were upheld. Unfortunately, these voluntary export restraints proved to be even more economically wasteful for the United States than tariffs. Under both a tariff and a VER consumers lose due to the higher prices, but the government collects a tax when it uses a tariff. With the VER, the government gets no tariff revenues. The Japanese auto producers got a higher price for their autos and avoided the tax, a much better outcome for the Japanese than under a tariff.

George W. Bush was less subtle in imposing steel tariffs in 2003 in hopes of swaying steelworkers' votes in hotly contested Ohio in 2004. It worked. Ohio went for Bush. If Ohio hadn't, John Kerry would have been elected president. The new buzzwords in international protectionism are "antidumping duties." "Dumping" occurs if a manufacturer sells a product abroad for a lower price than it sells for in its domestic market or if the product is sold below cost. No one likes to be "dumped on," and this is the new rallying cry for those seeking "protection."

In the first eleven years of the twenty-first century, the United States has incurred a substantial trade deficit, importing many more goods and services than it exported. In 2010, this imbalance reached nearly $500 billion. China held

las. http://www.dallasfed.org/assets/documents/fed/annual/2002/ar02.pdf .

the top spot in our trade deficit as we imported $273 billion more in Chinese goods and services than we exported to China. This imbalance makes China a popular congressional whipping boy for the U.S. trade deficit, although, as we show in our chapter on deficit spending, China is not to blame for our overall trade deficit.

Summing Up

Hawley-Smoot miserably failed to fulfill its goal of putting the United States "on the up-grade financially, economically, and commercially." Its tariffs imposed net losses for society that usually arise from restraint in trade (winners won less than losers lost), and it failed to increase aggregate spending and employment by attempting to beggar thy neighbors. The act also triggered ill will toward the United States and set nation against nation in a trade war that helped to set the stage for World War II. As the letter by U.S. economists sadly prophesized: "A tariff war does not furnish good soil for the growth of world peace." All told, the act is a worthy chapter in this book.

Next up, one of the biggest Ponzi-type schemes in U.S. history and a wreck that will be with us well into the twenty-first century: Social Security.

4

Social Security

America's Greatest Ponzi Scheme?

"[A] . . . full reserve [for Social Security] is unnecessary . . .
[A full reserve is a] monster, a leech particularly on the present
generation and . . . a menace to sound public finance, [the taxes
needed to finance it are] . . . a colossal imposition."
—*Senator Arthur Vandenberg* (R-MI)[1], 1939

IN LATE 1919, Carlo Ponzi began telling friends and family
members around Boston that he had discovered a way to make a 100 percent return on his money in a few months. Many wanted a chance at such easy money
and invested some of their savings with Ponzi in exchange for a written promise
that he would provide a 50 percent return on their investment in ninety days.
When the initial investors were paid off, they of course wanted to invest even
more. As word got around, many more people wanted a piece of the action. In
a few months, Ponzi was taking in more than $200,000 a day from investors,
promising to return their investment plus 50 percent in ninety days.

Was all this too good to be true? Of course, it was. Ponzi was not earning
anything for his investors as a group. He was simply taking money from new
investors and paying off people who had invested with him ninety days earlier.
In mid-1920, a Boston newspaper published an expose on Ponzi that panicked
his investors. Thousands stormed his office demanding to be paid off. But Ponzi
had only a small fraction of what had been invested. The rest had already been
paid out to previous investors or had been squandered by the big-spending

---

1. The Congressional Record, Vol. 84, part 1, 1939, 359–360.

Ponzi. The house of cards came crashing down. Many investors lost their life savings, and Ponzi eventually went to prison. Now such financial strategies are called Ponzi schemes. Recently, Bernie Madoff made headlines running a similar Ponzi scheme. Undoubtedly, there will be more in the future.

Ponzi's illegal venture seems insignificant when compared to Social Security, the federal retirement program for the elderly and disabled, one of the biggest Ponzi-type schemes the United States has ever seen.[2] We can see the Ponzi-like nature of this federal program most dramatically by considering the case of Ida Fuller, one of the very first Social Security recipients. Ida retired in 1940 at age 65, after having paid (or "invested") all of $22 in Social Security taxes. Her first monthly check was $22.54. She lived to age 100 and collected more than $21,000 in Social Security benefits. Ida got a far greater return on her investment than Ponzi promised his investors. How was Ida's unbelievable return in the Social Security program possible? It was made so by other taxpayers (or investors) who put up the money for her, just as later investors in Ponzi's scheme put up the money to pay off earlier investors. Common to both Ponzi's scheme and Social Security is that investors' funds are, for the most part, never invested but rather passed along to current recipients of Social Security to consume or do with as they wish.

Social Security differs from a "true" Ponzi scheme in two important respects. First, no fraud is involved. While Ponzi hid his misuse of investors' monies, the government unashamedly reports its financial transactions and missing funds. Second, the federal government can do something that Ponzi couldn't. When the true nature of Ponzi's scheme was exposed, he was unable to attract new investors, and the scheme collapsed abruptly. In contrast, the federal government so far has had little trouble forcing people to pay the taxes necessary to cover the promised benefits to Social Security retirees. So, to call Social Security a Ponzi scheme isn't correct. It is more correctly called a Ponzi-type scheme or—among those sympathetic to the idea—an "unfunded retirement program." But before discussing problems that lay ahead and the serious costs that Social Security imposes on society, we need to learn a bit more about the Social Security program.

---

2. Chapter 6 details an even bigger Ponzi-type scheme: the retirement health-care program, Medicare.

A Brief Overview

Social Security is a child of the Great Depression: The federal government gave birth to it in 1935.[3] Under its original design, Social Security was to provide old-age benefits to covered workers in commerce and industry, representing only about 50 percent of all workers. In 1939, even before the first dollar of benefits was paid, the program was expanded to provide benefits for dependents of retired workers and for surviving dependents. Disability insurance benefits, payable as early as age 50, were added in 1956. In the 1950s, coverage was extended to other previously excluded workers, making it essentially universal. Finally, medical insurance (Medicare) benefits were added in 1965. This chapter focuses only on Social Security and saves a discussion of Medicare for another chapter.

In the last sixty years, the program has grown from a small retirement program into a gargantuan check-writing machine that plays a central role in American life. In 1940, Social Security paid benefits to a quarter million people. Today more than 55 million people—about 18 percent of all Americans—receive a monthly Social Security retirement or disability check. The number of beneficiaries will surge to many more millions as the baby boom generation (those born post World War II in the 1946 to 1964 period) retires in the early years of this century. The Social Security Administration predicts 70 million beneficiaries by 2020, 86 million by 2030, and 93 million by 2040—or about 27 percent of all Americans.

As the number of beneficiaries has grown, so has the real purchasing power of their checks. From an initial maximum of $782 a month (2010 prices) in 1940, benefits at full retirement age have surged three-fold to $2,347 a month in 2011. In the late 1960s and early 1970s, Congress and the Nixon Administration were especially eager to raise benefits, and they were increased far faster than prices in general: 13 percent in 1968, 15 percent in 1970, 10 percent in 1971, 20 percent in 1972, and 11 percent in 1974. Since 1975, subsequent benefits have been tied to the Consumer Price Index (CPI), assuring that they will rise by at least as much as inflation each year.[4]

---

3. It was created as part of a sweeping piece of legislation that also established the federal unemployment compensation program and committed the federal government to sharing with the states the cost of welfare programs to aid the poor.

4. Economists generally agree that the CPI overstates the true rate of inflation, so Social Security beneficiaries actually receive annual benefit increases that exceed the inflation rate.

In 2010, Social Security outlays were nearly $750 billion, making it essentially tied for the biggest federal program alongside national defense and the Medicare and Medicaid programs. Projections for 2012 show expenditures on Social Security exceeding outlays on national defense.

Social Security outlays have doubled in size relative to our gross domestic product (GDP; the production of goods and services) between 1960 and 2011, increasing from 2.4 percent to 4.8 percent. They will continue to grow as more baby boomers claim retirement or disability benefits. Projections by the Social Security Administration suggest that outlays will stabilize at about 6 percent of GDP around 2030.

In light of the enormous growth in expenditures, we should expect comparable growth in Social Security taxes. And that is precisely what we find. Workers and their employers nominally share the cost of Social Security taxes equally, but many economists agree that the actual tax burden falls mainly on workers. Half of the tax is deducted explicitly from their paychecks, whereas the other half is largely passed on to workers in the form of lower wages than they would have otherwise been paid. The combined Social Security tax rates have soared from their initial level of 2 percent of the first $3,000 of earnings to 12.4 percent of the first $110,100 of earnings in 2012. While the percentage rates have been stable since 1990, there is good reason to believe that they may begin to rise—perhaps sharply—as more baby boomers retire.

Higher Taxes, Broken Promises, or Bigger Deficits?

The Social Security system is riddled with problems. Undoubtedly, the biggest problem for society is that it is unfunded. Under most private pension plans, a person pays money into an account (for example, an IRA or a 401-K account) that invests in various financial assets that provide retirement income. Such a pension plan is said to be "funded." Social Security pensions are "unfunded." Social Security taxes are not saved and invested;[5] rather benefits to retirees are paid with taxes taken from today's workers.

---

5. Technically, some funds are kept in an "SS Trust Fund," but these are far less than needed to qualify as a funded system.

Notably, Social Security was designed initially as a largely funded (called a "full reserve" plan) retirement program. Had it been fully funded, we would have avoided all of the problems that we now face. The original plan was that people would save by paying into the Social Security Trust Fund. Interest would be paid on the accumulated balances. On retirement, a person would receive benefits based on what that person had paid into the fund. Essentially, it was designed much like a funded private retirement program.[6] An exception was made for those retiring in the early years of the program. Since the early wave of retirees had paid relatively little in taxes, their pension checks would have been correspondingly small, had Social Security payouts been based strictly on their contributions. Many people might think this would have been fair. After all, prior to Social Security, people were responsible for saving for their own retirement, and people like Ida Fuller had a lifetime to save privately for their retirement. Nonetheless, the plan called for the early retirees to get much more than their tax payments could have justified. Excessive payments to retirees continued for decades while tax rate increases were delayed; little wonder Social Security was hailed as such a success and was so wildly popular in its first decades. Future retirees and taxpayers, as we will see, will not be so fortunate or likely to be as enthusiastic about Social Security.

The original funded arrangement for Social Security was converted to a *pay-as-you-go* system (that is, a Ponzi-type unfunded scheme) in 1939. Support for this switch was bipartisan and strongly supported by business lobby groups. Republicans were especially jubilant over the move to an unfunded program. The main driving force was a desire to avoid the scheduled tax increases on workers and especially on businesses needed to keep the system funded. Remarks by Senator Arthur Vandenberg (R-Mich.) illustrate the negative attitude toward a fully funded system.[7] He stated that a ". . . full reserve [for Social Security] is unnecessary. . . . [Full reserve is a] monster, a leech on society, and . . . a menace

---

6. There was an important difference between the original SS funding arrangement and most private pension plans. Private plans usually invest in stocks and bonds. Social Security was required—and still is—to invest all excess funds in federal bonds; that is, Social Security had to lend the money to the federal government.

7. The "full reserve" was something less than "fully funded." The Congressional Record, Vol. 84, part 1, 1939, 359–360.

to sound public finance. And the taxes needed to finance it are . . . a colossal imposition."[8]

By eliminating the requirement that the program be funded, the government could hold taxes down, at least for a while. For example, the combined tax rate (on workers and employers) was scheduled to rise from 2 percent to 3 percent in 1940 and eventually increase to 6 percent in 1949. But by switching to a pay-as-you-go system, the increase to 3 percent was postponed for ten years, and the increase to 6 percent was put off until 1960. Furthermore, without the need to fully fund the system, benefits could be increased and paid out earlier—and they were. This is clearly an example of politicians and lobbying groups suffering from *immediosis* (See Introduction)—focusing on short-run benefits and ignoring potential long-run problems: lower taxes and higher benefits now in exchange for problems in future generations. The longer run would be someone else's problem.

Taxing workers to pay for others' retirement benefits worked smoothly as long as the number of workers was considerably larger than the number of retirees. But once the baby-boom generation begins retiring, greatly reducing the number of workers per retiree, the Ponzi-like nature of Social Security will be painfully obvious. The ratio of workers per retiree has been stable at about 3.2 since the early 1970s, but official forecasts show it beginning to drop soon, falling to around 2.1 by 2030. Clearly, this demographic shift—35 percent fewer workers per retiree—will put considerable pressure on Social Security. Some sort of major change seems inevitable: (a) taxes will rise (perhaps sharply), (b) benefits will be cut, (c) the federal government will need to borrow even larger sums, or (d) a combination of these three approaches will be applied.

Since the mid-1980s, Social Security has taken in about $2.6 trillion more than it has paid out in benefits. And it will take in another $1 trillion or so in anticipation of the retirement of the baby-boom generation. Yet, even with these huge current surpluses, the federal government's best estimate is that the Social Security old age and survivors' insurance (OASI) trust fund will be exhausted in 2038 (although the disability trust fund will, under current law, be exhausted by 2020).

---

8. The Congressional Record, Vol. 84, part 1, 1939, 359–60.

Another way to look at the tax shortfall is to consider the unfunded liability currently faced by Social Security. The unfunded liability is the difference between (1) the present value of the future benefits promised to retirees and (2) the present value of the Social Security taxes that are expected to be collected under current law. The shortfall in tax revenue exceeds $16 trillion.[9] This is an amount about equal to our current national debt and one year's GDP.

Notably this projected shortfall occurs even after accounting for a substantial cut in benefits for most future retirees. Beginning in 2000, the age for qualifying for full benefits began to rise, reaching 66 years of age in 2005 and 67 years in 2022. A 65-year-old male has a life expectancy of about eighteen more years. So a person who would have retired at age 65 between 2005 and 2022 will have to wait another year or more for full benefits. That represents a 5.5 percent (= 1/18) cut in benefits for the average male retiree. Of course, those retiring in 2022 or later face an average cut in benefits equal to 11 percent (= 1/9), assuming life expectancy remains unchanged.[10]

Social Security as a Welfare Redistribution Program

Unlike a private, fully funded retirement program that pays retirement monies closely linked to the amount of money paid into the retirement plan, Social Security has allowed our elected federal officials to build a nontransparent welfare element into the program.[11] For example, lower income retirees receive proportionately more benefits relative to their taxes paid—sometimes a lot more—than higher income retirees. A person retiring in 2012, for example, whose last year of income was $12,000 (and earlier years estimated) would receive

---

9. "2010 OASDI Trustees Report," retrieved from http://ssa.gov/oact/TR/2010/IV_LRest.html. This is the infinite horizon estimate. This uses a discounting procedure for future years and carries the calculations infinitely far into the future. Due to the discounting procedure, years far out, say 100 years, receive very little weight.

10. If life expectancy increases, the percentage reduction in benefits would be smaller. However, increases in life expectancy may well provide the rationale for pushing the Social Security retirement age back further.

11. The decision about when and how to take Social Security benefits is much more complicated than most people understand. Several services and websites now exist that help make these decisions. One of the best: http://www.socialsecuritychoices.com/index.php.

about $606 in monthly benefits; an individual earning $48,000 (and earlier years estimated) in her last year would receive about $1,308.[12] The higher income individual would have contributed four times more in tax contributions but receive only slightly more than double the monthly benefit of the lower income individual.

Social Security also redistributes according to marital status. Since a married couple theoretically needs more in retirement, Social Security gives married couples a bonus even if only one partner worked outside the home and paid Social Security taxes. For example, a single man retiring in 2011 can expect $266,000 in total benefits, having paid into the system $305,000.[13] A married couple with the same wage income and only one worker paying taxes would have paid the same in taxes as the single man but receive an expected $453,000 in benefits.

The intergenerational redistributions that Social Security has made, as previously illustrated in the case of Ida Fuller, also can be illustrated in the following examples for single women having earned average wages, retiring at age 65, but in different retirement years. In 1960, she had paid a total of $18,000 in taxes (all numbers, again, in 2011 dollars) but could expect $146,000 in benefits. Retiring in 1980, she would have paid in $96,000 and could expect to receive $249,000. By 2011, the benefit-tax relationship reverses: She has paid $299,000 in taxes and receives only $290,000 in expected benefits. Her retirement fund has lost money in real terms over her working life. And the expected losses get worse beyond 2011. The earlier retirees did so well in large part due to the transitioning from a fully funded system to a pay-as-you-go system. Now the single people will experience losses—that's how the single-worker married couple gets its "bonus."

Welfare payments or income redistribution programs may or may not be socially desirable. Regardless, to disguise such a large redistribution program as part of a retirement program is a real problem. The redistribution element

---

12. Computed from the Social Security website: http://www.ssa.gov/OACT/quickcalc/index.html.

13. All of the numbers used in the following illustrations have been converted into 2011 dollars and use a 2 percent real interest rate. This conclusion also assumes an average wage over the working lifetime. Source: Steuerle and Rennane, 2011.

in Social Security is largely nontransparent and not well understood by the typical citizen, allowing lawmakers tremendous latitude in the redistribution of income without public debate over the welfare issues.

Other Equity Issues?

Since Social Security was initiated, there has been a substantial change in labor markets. Today, many more households have two income earners paying two separate sets of taxes. A household with two average-income earners will pay double the taxes of a household of two adults where only one works outside the home for an average salary. The two-income family retiring in 2011 can expect $560,000 in benefits; the one-income family will receive $453,000 in benefits. So, the two-income family pays 100 percent more in taxes but receives only 24 percent more in benefits. Worse yet for the two-income family, its tax contributions are greater than the benefits it expects to receive (all in 2011 dollars); the one-income family picks up close to $150,000 more in benefits than they paid in taxes. Partners in the two-income family also likely incur more costs during their working lives, paying more for household cleaning services, child-care, and so on than the one-income family. Some people might find this payoff rule unfair.

One of my favorite Social Security payoff rules was brought to my attention by a colleague who calls it the "trophy bride rule." Consider the case of an old geezer on Social Security having earned $100,000 in his last year before retiring. After retiring, he marries a young woman and adopts her child (or perhaps they have one of their own). The old geezer continues to collect his $2,098 in monthly SS benefits, but he now gets an additional $1,049 monthly for his child until the child reaches age 18.[14] If the couple has more children, benefits would be higher although there is a cap on total benefits. Furthermore, the young bride who may never work a day in her life outside the home and may never pay a penny in taxes will qualify for widow benefits, should the geezer pass on before she reaches retirement age. Furthermore, she will receive 100 percent of her (presumably) dead husband's benefits when she reaches retirement age.

---

14. From SS website: http://www.ssa.gov/OACT/quickcalc/index.html.

Those finding the above example sexist can substitute "cougar" for "geezer" and reverse the sex of the spouse.

Social Security and National Savings

Arguably the worst problem of Social Security has been saved for last: There is evidence that Social Security has substantially reduced the nation's savings. But, before getting into the details, let's see why savings matters.

The after-tax income our economy generates each year can be used in two ways: we can spend it on goods and services or we can save it. An important benefit from saving is that some portion of it goes into lending through financial markets to support business and government investments (e.g., for plant and equipment by businesses or highways and school buildings by governments). Productive investments by business or government enhance our economy's ability to produce goods and services in the future; that is, they help the economy to grow and prosper. Thus, reducing savings reduces the available funds to support business and government investment and ultimately lowers the standard of living we all enjoy.

Why would Social Security alter savings? Because many look at Social Security taxes as savings that will help fund retirement. But we have seen that the taxes aren't saved—they were passed on to people like Ida Fuller, who was able to consume more and retire earlier than her own savings would have permitted. Social Security taxes and promised benefits lead people to conclude that they can retire earlier and do not need to save as much privately to achieve their retirement objectives. So, the Social Security system to some extent substitutes for and reduces personal savings. While the amount of substitution has yet to be firmly established by economists, it is likely to be in the trillions of dollars. Martin Feldstein, a prominent economist at Harvard University and director of the National Bureau for Economic Research, reports findings suggesting that Social Security has reduced private savings by as much as 60 percent. Notably, personal savings as a percentage of disposable income, until the recession that started in 2008, had been declining fairly steadily since 1975.

Social Security wealth adds nothing to U.S. productive capacity. It is merely a promise to tax someone in the future. Private savings and private wealth add to a nation's productive capacity; Social Security taxes and Social Security wealth do not. Private savings provide funding to nurture the building of industry and give society the capital needed to become affluent.

How much of an impact on our standard of living could such a savings reduction cause? This depends on the magnitude of the reduction in real private savings and wealth that has occurred. Economists are unlikely to agree on an exact number, but we can be fairly confident that it is in the trillions of dollars. Given that the value of capital for all companies listed on stock exchanges hovers around $20 trillion, even a $2 trillion reduction in capital would be a substantial reduction in our capital stock and in our productive capacity. The actual number could be much more.

A reduction in savings by Americans need not necessarily lower available capital in the United States, but it can lead to a change in who owns the capital. If reduced domestic savings are replaced by foreign funds, a negative impact on the amount of capital in the United States can be avoided. Indeed, the United States has experienced a net inflow of foreign investment every year since 1976. Current total foreign investment in the United States exceeds $5 trillion, up from $2.5 trillion just ten years ago. Some of this investment is financial in nature (e.g., buying stocks and bonds). This gives foreigners ownership rights to U.S. companies and gives foreigners substantial claims on dividends and interest. Some of the foreigners invest by purchasing real estate and other property. Japanese investors own the Bank of California, and for a time they owned Rockefeller Center in New York City. The list of U.S. businesses or other assets controlled by foreign investors is undoubtedly a lengthy one. So to some extent, our reduced domestic savings associated with Social Security has attracted foreign savings. Thus, our pay-as-you-go system has facilitated the mortgaging of the United States to foreigners, or the sale of U.S. assets to foreigners. Bad as all this seems, what might be called "the mother" of all pay-as-you-go systems is saved for a later chapter.

Final Remarks

This chapter ends on a pessimistic note. The problems created by Social Security have been recognized for more than three decades, but they have not been resolved as yet, and they will not be resolved easily. As Al Ullman, chairperson of the U.S. House Ways and Means Committee, said more than three decades ago (in 1977):

> There is no such thing as an easy way out of the social security dilemma. There are not going to be any more easy votes on social security . . . Those who would tell us that there is some easy way to solve the social security problem are not telling us the way it is.[15]

We are mired in this difficult mess as a result of interactions among at least six factors:

1. Politicians' short-run orientation (immediosis).
2. A large, growing, and politically influential special interest group (Social Security beneficiaries and those approaching retirement), which has been successful in expanding benefits in the past and strongly resists any benefit reductions.
3. A tax burden that was low—especially during the first several decades of Social Security's existence—because the number of beneficiaries was small relative to the many tens of millions of taxpayers. This led to excessive increases in benefits.
4. Taxpayers not understanding that they bear most, if not all, of the combined Social Security tax burden. This has weakened taxpayer resistance to higher taxes.
5. The population bulge created by the baby-boom generation.
6. The foolish idea, held even by some academic economists, that the pay-as-you-go system is a "free lunch."

The last item was clearly articulated by Senator Vandenberg, who viewed the taxes and accumulated funds needed to have a full reserve for Social Security as a "menace" and a "colossal imposition" on the economy. Imagine applying the same logic to all private retirement accounts—just substitute "savings" for "taxes": "[A] . . . full reserve [for your private retirement account] is unnecessary. . . . [Your savings is a] monster, a leech on society, and . . . a menace to sound

---

15. As quoted in Sheryl R. Tynes, 1996, *Turning Points in Social Security* (Stanford, CA: Stanford University Press).

public finance. And the [savings] needed to finance it are . . . a colossal imposition." Following such logic eventually would turn any developed economy into one as affluent as Zimbabwe.

The interaction among the six factors was especially evident between 1968 and 1974, when benefits were increased five separate times, four of them in election years. It is surely no coincidence that during this period, many millions of baby boomers were entering the labor force,[16] providing an infusion of Social Security taxes, which politicians were happy to convert into larger benefit checks that beneficiaries were even happier to receive.

Of course, a retiring baby-boom generation will push Social Security into bankruptcy under current law. And, as the number of Social Security beneficiaries swells by many more millions, they will become an even more politically powerful group. Future benefit reductions will become even harder to make. As the statement by Congressman Ullman notes, cutting benefits has long been a politically dangerous thing to do. For many years Social Security has been referred to as the "third rail" of American politics: like the electrified third rail of some subway systems, touch it and you're dead (politically).

It is usually a safe bet that politicians will follow the line of least resistance. Eventually, they will have to choose between raising taxes substantially, slashing benefits (in part by delaying retirement age), or borrowing trillions of dollars (or some combination thereof). Raising public indebtedness will become increasingly more dangerous and difficult, so higher taxes and benefit cuts are reasonable predictions. As bad as Social Security is financially, a sustainable solution is feasible, but it is almost politically impossible to re-establish a fully funded system. The tax increases and benefit cuts needed to make the system fully funded are immense. And as bad as the problem is, it is minor compared to the problems posed by Medicare.

Next up, our wasteful tax system.

---

16. High school-educated boomers began entering the labor force in 1964, with the initial wave of college-educated boomers following in 1968. Between 1964 and 1974, the civilian labor force grew by 18 million people. Most of this increase reflects the entry of baby boomers into the labor force. (About 2.5 million is attributable to an increase in the labor force participation rate, especially among women.) By contrast, in the ten years prior to 1964, the labor force grew by only 8.8 million people.

5

Tax Follies
The 91-Percent Solution

"The Power to tax is the power to destroy."
—*Chief Justice John Marshall* in the Supreme Court case,
McCulloch v. Maryland

SUGAR RAY ROBINSON (b. 1921–d. 1989) was arguably the greatest boxer pound-for-pound the world has ever seen and possibly the best boxer of all time. During his boxing career, Sugar Ray earned over $4 million in purse money, a grand fortune during his peak earning years, the late 1940s and the 1950s. And Mr. Robinson really earned it. He fought more than 200 professional fights and won 173 of them. He had been a welterweight champion and then a middleweight champion, losing and regaining the middleweight title an incredible four times. During his boxing years, he also became a philanthropist and an entrepreneur who owned numerous properties in New York City's Harlem, including a trendy restaurant-night club frequented by many stars including Frank Sinatra and Dean Martin. At the end of his life, he suffered from boxers' dementia, lived off the generosity of friends, especially Frank Sinatra, and died in relative poverty.[1]

Mr. Robinson clearly had an extravagant lifestyle. He earned large, and he spent large. When he traveled, he traveled in style and with a large number of friends and assistants. On one of his trips to France, the press referred to his

---

1. For an excellent film documentary of Sugar Ray Robinson's life, see "Sugar Ray Robinson: The Bright Lights and Dark Shadows of a Champion," available at http://www.youtube.com/watch?v=kfYCdyvF45E.

traveling companions as his "entourage." The word is now common usage in English. But Mr. Robinson had other financial drains: a property manager who caused $250,000 to disappear and, even more costly, the Internal Revenue Service (IRS). His IRS debt was so large that most of his boxing revenues after 1952 went to paying current and back taxes. Mr. Robinson never recovered financially.

While many factors contributed to Mr. Robinson's financial demise, including self-inflicted problems, a look at the tax rates that he faced helps to put the IRS's role into perspective. In Mr. Robinson's prime, marginal tax rates were at their U.S. historical peak. For example, in 1951, as a married person filing jointly, any of his earnings over $32,000 was taxed at 50 percent, and the rates went up for every additional $10,000 in earnings. The marginal rate for earnings over $300,000 was 91 percent. Fortunately for Mr. Robinson, there was a Mrs. Robinson, or the 91-percent tax bracket would have kicked in at $150,000.

Mr. Robinson fought an incredible eleven bouts in 1951. In his first fight, he moved up in weight division to defeat Jake LaMatta and capture the world middleweight title. In his last two fights, he lost and then regained the title against Randy Turpin; his total purses for these last two fights reportedly were in excess of $250,000. Sugar Ray might not have known it at the time, but he was soon to become a victim of his own excessive productivity. His last fights in 1951 quite likely pushed him into the 91 percent federal tax bracket. In essence, his last fights in 1951 probably netted him only nine cents on the dollar less any income taxes due the State of New York. But in 1952, after losing the middleweight title, Mr. Robinson figured he had earned enough and retired from boxing. He figured wrong.

In 1955, after a three-year retirement, Mr. Robinson reentered the ring and earned $231,000 in his first two fights. Even if he was able to deduct half of this amount for business expenses, the next dollar he earned was subject to the 75 percent federal income tax. But he saw almost none of his first two purses in 1955 as the IRS seized $171,000 immediately to pay for back taxes. All told, the IRS took from Mr. Robinson far more than his unscrupulous property manager stole. Mr. Robinson fell into a deep financial hole, and an outrageously expropriating tax code helped to put him there. As Chief Justice Marshall wrote, the power to tax is also the power to destroy.

If Mr. Robinson had boxed between 1990 and 2012, his tax burden would have been far less onerous and, if he had been more judicious with his earnings (including using a good tax attorney), he would have lived out a prosperous life. Regardless, it was still his money, and he had every right to use it any way he desired.

While marginal tax rates are now lower than during the Robinson boxing years, the rates and other provisions in the tax code continue to do substantial damage to the U.S. economy, and due to various loopholes in the tax code, these rates are much higher than they need to be. Worse yet, these tax rates and the damage they produce are likely to rise substantially in the future. The power to tax is not only the power to destroy but also the power to produce economic waste. The inefficiencies caused by the existing tax code make it one of our biggest economic wrecks. Revising the tax code to improve the functioning of the U.S. economy is one of our greatest challenges in the twenty-first century.

Fair and Efficient Taxes: Are They Possible?

Taxes distort, and these distortions produce economic waste. Taxes distort the prices we pay and the incomes we receive. Economists conclude that, in the overwhelming majority of cases, these tax distortions cause economic inefficiencies and a net loss to society.[2] Let's construct a simple example to help illustrate this point. Assume you decide to buy a new automobile. The one you select costs $15,000, but you think it is well worth it—worth at least $18,000 to you (the $3,000 value to you in excess of the price is called *consumer surplus* by economists). But before you can buy the car, the government places a $5,000 tax on automobiles that pushes the total price of your preferred car above $18,000. You decide that buying a new car is no longer worth it. The tax distorts your decision and leaves you worse off as you no longer get consumer surplus from buying the car at the pre-tax price. Although the government has placed a tax on new cars, it fails to get any tax from you, a discouraged car buyer. In this simple case, the

---

2. A tax can correct a market failure. Goods that do not include the pollution costs in their production costs erroneously give a price that is too cheap—below true costs—to consumers. A tax in this case could correct a pre-existing market distortion.

net economic loss associated with your distorted decision is your loss of consumer surplus. Your tax leaves you worse off by $3,000—it prevents you from getting $3,000 in consumer surplus—and no one else, including the government is better off, as a result of your loss.

What if you had valued the car at $25,000? The tax would not distort your decision, and no net economic loss occurs. Here's why. Let's assume the price of the car rises from $15,000 to $20,000 as a result of the tax, and you buy it. You would have had $10,000 in consumer surplus, if the tax had not raised the price, but you still receive $5,000 in consumer surplus. While you have lost $5,000 in consumer surplus, the government and, in essence, taxpayers, gain $5,000 in tax revenues from you. For society as a whole, if the tax does not distort a decision, it becomes a transfer of benefits from one person or group to another: The government gains in revenues what you lose.

This example is highly simplified. In general, taxes are usually shared to some extent by both the sellers and buyers, and some potential buyers refrain from making purchases as a result of taxes. Taxes on a good or service not only can raise its price to the buyer but also can lower the after-tax price received by the seller. Income taxes on wages likely do this. Income taxes are a tax on another kind of product, services that provide income to their owners. These services come from labor, land, and capital. The sale of these services gives their owners wages, rent, interest, and profits. Income taxes on wages decrease the price received by workers (the sellers of labor services) and increase the wages paid by employers (the buyers of labor services), causing distortions that produce losses as in the auto-tax example.[3] Taxes on wages might lead some workers, especially those who are of retirement age and second-income earners, to drop out of the labor force to work on household chores. Others might "go underground" and work for cash to avoid taxes altogether.

One important finding in the study of taxation is that the net economic loss usually increases faster than the tax rate. Returning to the auto example, doubling the tax from $5,000 to $10,000 can be expected to more than double the net loss to society, as many more potential car buyers will be discouraged, and

---

3. Economists figure that most of the burden from wage taxes falls on the workers in the form of lower take-home pay.

losses in consumer surplus will be larger to the additional discouraged buyers. *To reduce economic waste, economists usually favor the lowest tax rate possible to create the smallest possible distortion. To achieve this, they recommend the biggest (broadest) tax base possible.* The tax base is the monetary value of the wealth item or income activity being taxed. For any given total tax revenue needed, the broadest tax base permits the lowest tax rate.

Economists look for taxes that might not produce a net loss to society, but these taxes are hard to find and often politically unsellable. One such impractical tax is a lump-sum tax. For example, tax everyone $10,000 a year regardless of income. This turns out to be efficient, as it avoids price distortions, but most people think it unfair.[4] Other taxes that might not produce net losses are taxes that "correct" market-pricing failures. One such tax would be a pollution tax that more correctly forces the price of the product to reflect the true cost of its production. Other taxes that likely don't distort much and therefore don't cause much economic loss are taxes on such things as cigarettes and alcohol. Drinkers and smokers are unlikely to give up their bad habits. These types of taxes, even if properly implemented, are too insignificant to be an adequate source of revenue for financing large governments. Thus, we are stuck with turning to inefficient taxes, but with an idea about how to minimize their economic damage: use the biggest tax base and apply the lowest tax rate possible to finance the size of government that we desire.

Among the biggest tax bases is our national income, the sum of all of our wages, salaries, interest, rent, and profit.[5] For 2010, U.S. national income was about $14.5 trillion. So, within the United States, there was roughly $14.5 trillion in reported wages, salaries, interest, rent, and profit. The actual number is undoubtedly larger because the official numbers do not include any "underground" economy activities such as unreported cash payments for work and implicit wages received from work done at home on such things as household

---

4. Such a tax would lead to changes in prices for items as the differential effects on people's disposable incomes would lead to changes in the demand for various goods. These income-affected price changes do not cause inefficiency and net losses to society.

5. Technically, the dollar value of GDP and national income will differ because GDP includes payments for depreciation of capital and some indirect taxes that do not get counted as income.

chores and child-rearing. But national income is among the broadest tax bases we have.

In addition to a tax on national income, other taxes that use big tax bases would include a value-added tax (VAT), a general sales tax, and a consumption tax. A VAT puts a tax at each stage of production but only on the value added (arising from new costs due to wages and salaries, interest, rent, and profit) at each stage. VATs usually exempt investment in plant and equipment so it is considered a consumption tax. Since consumption is the largest use for our national income, a VAT uses a large tax base.

Another tax that uses a large tax base and holds the potential for little distortion is a tax on the value of unimproved land. Popularized by the nineteenth-century writer and economist Henry George, the tax would not apply to any improvements to the land, so development of the land would not be penalized with the tax. Land taxes that include taxes on improvements are popular revenue sources for local governments, but a federal tax on the value of unimproved land values has never caught on. Some economists have noted that an unimproved land tax, if set too high, might cause distortions by removing incentives to own land.

While it is difficult to find an efficient tax, is it any easier to find a "fair" tax? Of course it is, just ask anyone—they'll tell you what a fair tax is. Unfortunately, we can't reach much agreement because value judgments enter into these assessments. Some people, in reading about Sugar Ray's financial problems, might conclude that he was being taxed fairly, whereas others would disagree. My earlier conclusion that the tax rates he faced were unduly high reveals my own evaluation. Most people think that it is fair for wealthier or higher income people to pay more taxes, but how much more is "fair"? If someone earns twice as much income as you do, should he or she pay twice as much in taxes? Four times as much? Ten times as much? There is no objective answer to which of these, if any, is "fair."

Our current tax code in 2012 is economically wasteful and unfair in many respects. It is possible to make it less wasteful and fairer, at least according to most people's value judgments, but the politician's golden rule—to provide benefits now and to delay or hide costs—stands in the way. We now look at some of the specific blunders caused by our personal and corporate income taxes.

Income Taxes

The 16th Amendment to the Constitution, passed in 1913, made the income tax a permanent fixture of the U.S. tax system. Previously, the federal government relied heavily on excise taxes (specific sales taxes on such things as the sale of alcohol) and tariffs on imports. These taxes fell relatively heavily on lower income people, and the income tax provided an opportunity to shift the tax burden more toward higher income earners.[6] Once the amendment gave Congress the power to tax individual and corporate income, Congress moved quickly. While the U.S. government had imposed income taxes earlier, for example, to assist in financing the Civil War, these taxes were merely temporary. Income taxes were now here to stay.

The 1913 personal income tax was quite simple: three pages of forms and one page of instructions. Table 5.1 shows the various tax rates that applied to individuals in 1913. An individual or married couple earning taxable income under $20,000 ($458,000 in 2011 dollars) paid only 1 percent of their income in taxes. Even then, the tax rates were *graduated*, that is, higher tax rates were applied to different ranges or brackets of *additional* income (the rates applied to additional amounts of income are called *marginal* tax rates). The highest marginal rate, 7 percent, applied only to any income earned in excess of $500,000 ($11.45 million in 2011 dollars).[7]

Income taxes today are considerably more complicated, less transparent, and certainly more costly. There are now more than 500 separate tax forms and more than 7,000 pages of tax preparation instructions. In 2009, the IRS estimated that between 900,000 and 1.2 million paid tax preparers to help hapless taxpayers through the morass of tax rules.[8] Table 5.2 presents the tax brackets and rates applicable for taxable income in 2011. In the future, these tax brackets will automatically adjust to compensate for inflation, which pushes up incomes

---

6. John Steele Gordon, "A Short History of the Income Tax," *The Wall Street Journal*, Tuesday, September 27, 2011, A15.

7. For a copy of the original 1913 tax form and instructions, go to http://www.irs.gov/pub/irs-utl/1913.pdf.

8. "Return Preparer Review," December 2009, Internal Revenue Service, Publication 4832 (Rev. 12-2009) Catalog Number 54419P. Retrieved from http://www.irs.gov/pub/irs-pdf/p4832.pdf.

Table 5.1. Marginal Tax Rates, 1913

Tax rates on taxable income (regardless of marital status)

	IN 1913 DOLLARS		IN 2011 DOLLARS	
Rate	Over	But not over	Over	But not over
1.0%	$0	$20,000	$0	$458,000
2.0%	$20,000	$50,000	$458,000	$1,145,000
3.0%	$50,000	$75,000	$1,145,000	$1,717,500
4.0%	$75,000	$100,000	$1,717,500	$2,290,000
5.0%	$100,000	$250,000	$2,290,000	$5,725,000
6.0%	$250,000	$500,000	$5,725,000	$11,450,000
7.0%	$500,000	—	$11,450,000	

Source: courtesy of Donald R. Johnson, Tax Foundation, and calculations of the author. www.taxfoundation.org.

Table 5.2. Marginal tax rates, 2011

Tax rates on taxable income (married filing jointly)

Rate	Over	But not over
10%	$0	$17,000
15%	$17,000	$69,000
25%	$69,000	$139,350
28%	$139,350	$212,300
33%	$212,300	$379,150
35%	$379,150	—

Source: courtesy of Donald R. Johnson and Tax Foundation. www.taxfoundation.org.

without increasing their real value. For example, given 10 percent inflation, the lowest bracket will adjust from $0 to $17,000 to $0 to $18,700. In 2011, the lowest income bracket for a married couple filing jointly was subject to a 10 percent tax rate. The highest tax bracket was for taxable income over $379,150, and the applicable tax rate was 35 percent. In 2012, the highest marginal rate was raised. Beginning in 2013, the marginal tax rate on income in excess of $450,000 for a married couple filing jointly is 39.6 percent. All other marginal tax rates would rise by 5 percent if the Bush temporary tax cuts passed in 2001 and 2003 ever expire. For example, the lowest income bracket will revert to 15 percent. These marginal tax rates do not include state income taxes and federal payroll taxes for Social Security and government health care. These additional taxes push the tax rates significantly higher, especially for income coming from wages and salaries.

From its inception, the federal income tax only applied to taxable income. Due to various deductions and *loopholes* in the tax code, many dollars in income are excluded from taxation when calculating taxable income. *In fact, today nearly half of all families pay no income tax at all.*[9]

All the factors that shrink the federal income tax base require that tax rates be higher than they otherwise need to be. They also disguise subsidy programs under a veil of tax reductions.

Tax Expenditures: Hidden Subsidy Programs

As with so many other terms in economics, the term *tax expenditures* isn't the most accurate way to describe the deductions, exemptions, and loopholes allowed in our tax code. A better name for these items might be hidden subsidy programs. An example helps to clarify. Let's assume we start with a simple income tax system that applies a 20 percent tax rate to all income from wages, salaries, interest, rent, and profits. Now, let's assume the government decides to subsidize people for "doing good." To provide a concrete example, let's assume doing good consists of donating a week of labor to a charity soup kitchen providing meals to the poor. Assume every time someone volunteers a week's work in the soup kitchen, he or she receives a $100 payment from the government. The outlays for paying people who volunteer in the soup kitchen will appear as an explicit outlay in the government's budget. Higher tax rates or more federal borrowing will be needed if other government spending programs remain unchanged.

Now consider the following alternative scheme. Again, assume that everyone faces a 20 percent income tax rate. Let's now allow everyone who works a week in the soup kitchen to deduct $500 from his or her income. If everyone

---

9. Many of these families do get hit by payroll taxes for Social Security and federal health care.

who works in the soup kitchen has enough income to take advantage of these deductions, the two programs are exactly equivalent, but with one major exception. The program using deductions does not appear in the government's budget, even though it provides exactly the same payout for volunteering in the soup kitchen as the explicit payment program. With an explicit subsidy, the volunteer gets a $100 check from the government. In the hidden subsidy case, the volunteer receives a $100 tax rebate. In either case, a volunteer who works one week in the soup kitchen receives a $100 subsidy. The government must raise tax rates or increase government borrowing by the same amount in either case.

Of course, people who do a lot of work in the soup kitchen may not get $100 in subsidy for every week's work, as deductions are only valuable if there is taxable income to subtract from. For example, if Sue has $1,500 in income and volunteers four weeks, she gets no subsidy for her last week's work. Also in a system where marginal tax rates are graduated, higher income earners with marginal tax rates higher than 20 percent will find the $500 deduction for working in the kitchen gives a greater subsidy than $100 per volunteer week. If Sam is in the 30 percent marginal tax bracket, he will get a $150 subsidy for each week at the kitchen (0.30 × $500). Some might question the fairness of a subsidy program that gives differential rewards to different do-gooders for doing the same amount of good.

Returning to the actual U.S. income tax, we merely need to substitute other words for weeks of work in the soup kitchen to discover our hidden subsidy programs—words such as: paying interest on mortgages, paying property and state income taxes, making 401-K contributions, receiving employer-sponsored health insurance, and receiving interest on state and local government bonds, to name just some of the most significant. The subsidies for these deductions do not appear as government outlays but are in fact equivalent to explicit subsidy programs. Some politicians mistakenly call these deductions "tax reductions" and consider their elimination a tax increase. The deductions are plain and simply subsidy programs. Is it reasonable to call the elimination of farm-crop subsidies or wind-power subsidies a tax increase? Elimination of a subsidy is an elimination of a subsidy, not a tax increase.

Most hidden subsidy programs have a ring of plausible acceptability: Homeowners need help in financing houses to achieve the American dream, state and

Table 5.3. Largest Tax Expenditures in Fiscal Year 2013 (in billions of dollars)

Provision	Amount
Exclusion for employer-sponsored health insurance	294.3
Mortgage interest deduction	100.9
401(k) plans	72.7
Lower rate on capital gains	62.0
EITC	55.7
Pensions	52.3
State and local tax deduction (excluding property tax)	46.3
Tax deferral for multi-nationals	41.8
Child tax credit	40.8
Charity deduction (other than education, health)	39.8

Source: U.S. Budget, Analytical Perspectives, FY2013. Courtesy of Leonard E. Burman.

local governments need help in financing their borrowing costs, and so on. But under closer examination, most of these activities do not improve economic efficiency or redistribute income in ways most people would consider fair. In any event, the hidden subsidies require that tax rates be much higher than they otherwise would be because they reduce the tax base.

How large are the hidden subsidy programs? Rather enormous. Table 5.3 provides information on estimates for the largest categories of tax expenditures. During fiscal year 2011, tax expenditures totaled nearly $1.2 trillion, an amount substantially larger than defense spending ($744 billion) or Medicare and Medicaid ($753 billion). If we add the tax expenditures into the federal budget, they would add about 33 percent to federal spending, and the percentage of our national income spent by the federal government would increase from 23.1 percent to 30.7 percent.

Why are tax expenditures so politically popular? Leonard Burman and Marvin Phaup in a National Bureau of Economic Research working paper sum it up succinctly: "In a nutshell, it is because sponsors of explicit spending may be attacked for favoring high taxes and big government. A similar tax expenditure program makes both taxes and spending appear lower, which offers obvious political advantages."[10] So tax expenditures allow politicians to subsidize their favored groups and to claim that they support "small" government, while hiding more than $1 trillion in subsidy programs.

Home Ownership Subsidies

One of the largest tax expenditure items is the interest deduction for home mortgages. In 2011, an estimated $104.5 billion of tax subsidies were handed out. Homeowners were also handed another $23.7 billion through deductions for property taxes and $31.3 billion in exclusions of capital gains on home sales. All of these subsidy programs have led to urban sprawl and inefficient overconsumption of housing. Someone who buys one or two McMansions receives a substantial tax subsidy that erodes the tax base.

The exclusion of capital gains from home sales encourages speculation in the housing market and provides substantial wealth benefits to those lucky enough to have a house that has gone up in value. One nice little scam to take advantage of the exclusion involves buying a "fixer-upper," doing the renovation and repairs yourself, and then selling the home after residing in it for two years. A couple can exclude $500,000 in capital gains from taxation. This loophole is particularly attractive for handymen and women and building contractors, who are able to convert their labor activities into tax-free income. If they fixed up a paying customer's home, their wage income would be fully subject to taxation, but doing the same work on their own homes avoids the tax.

These home-buying subsidies helped to fuel the housing boom and put households deeply into mortgage debt. This left homeowners at risk in the event of a housing-price downturn, as the bursting of the housing bubble from 2008 to 2012 has dramatically shown. Many of these houses are now "under water," worth less than the mortgages their buyers owe, causing financial distress for the owners and mortgage issuers alike. For many, the American dream of owning a home has turned into the American nightmare. Many Americans are now

---

10. The estimates for tax expenditures used in this chapter come from Leonard E. Burman and Marvin Phaup, "Tax Expenditures, the Size and Efficiency of Government, and Implications for Budget Reform," in Jeffrey Brown, ed., *Tax Policy and the Economy, Volume 26* (Chicago: University of Chicago Press, August 2012) 93–124.

discovering renting as a superior alternative to homeownership. Without the homeownership subsidies, they might never have forgotten about it.

Exclusion for Employer-Sponsored Health Insurance

The largest category of tax expenditure is the exclusion for employer-sponsored health insurance. Health insurance provided by an employer is an important and expensive employee benefit. The employer's cost is an implicit wage for the employee and can be worth many thousands of dollars each year to the individual. Moreover, it is better than wages because no one pays taxes on these hidden wages. If employers stopped paying insurance premiums and gave the money to employees, those dollars would be subject to income and payroll taxes. The subsidy given on employer-provided health insurance distorts the health care market and encourages employees to ask for more extensive and elaborate insurance than they might seek without the subsidy.

The exclusion of these benefits from taxation in fiscal year 2011 amounts to an estimated $177 billion annual subsidy to employees and employers offering health insurance.[11] This subsidy encourages a wasteful overconsumption of health insurance.[12]

Exclusion for Tax Exempt Bonds

State and local government bonds, called municipal bonds, provided nearly $29 billion in subsidies during fiscal year 2011. Owners of these bonds are able to exclude the interest income they receive from their bonds, thereby avoiding taxation. Because of the tax advantage these bonds offer, state and local governments can borrow at lower interest rates, so they receive some of the subsidy. The rest of the subsidy goes to buyers who benefit from the tax exemption, receiving a higher after-tax return than they would get from taxable bonds with similar risk. It turns out that the highest income-bracket taxpayers are the primary

---

11. As with most taxes and subsidies, the burden and benefits often get shared between buyers and sellers. For example, the firm offering health insurance may be able to hire workers at lower overall cost.

12. For example, due to the subsidy, "Cadillac" policies might be purchased while less comprehensive "Chevrolet" policies would be bought without the subsidy.

beneficiaries of municipal bonds. Most savers outside the top tax brackets will find that the higher interest paid on other bonds is more attractive, even after paying taxes. So, high-income people are the primary beneficiaries.[13] The very rich may have millions of dollars invested in municipal bonds and pay no income taxes at all on the interest income. In one well-publicized example, Teresa Heinz Kerry, wife of Senator John Kerry, reported earning about $5 million in income in 2003 with about $2.5 million coming from interest on state and local bonds. None of that $2.5 million was subject to any federal income tax.

Subsidizing the very rich and encouraging debt by state and local governments is a questionable subsidy program. In addition, we know that such tax expenditures lower the income tax base and require higher and more wasteful marginal income tax rates.

Excessive Taxation of Savings

Savings are crucial for long-run economic development. Countries with low savings rates have low standards of living, unless foreign countries step in and provide the capital needed for economic development. Current U.S. tax policy favors consumption over savings, and this reduces savings and impedes long-run U.S. development. How is the savings decision distorted? After income is earned and income taxes paid, the individual decides whether to consume or save. Those who save can anticipate substantially more taxation. If the money goes into a bank, the interest is treated as ordinary income and taxed at the marginal tax rate. If the money is invested in stocks, dividend and capital gains taxes apply. For those who use the funds, however, additional taxes are usually small, such as state-level sales taxes, or nonexistent. Imagine buying a product that gives you years of happiness. The flow of happiness goes untaxed. This is not true for savings. The future happiness obtained in the form of dividends, interest, or capital gains is taxed relatively heavily. This tax bias encourages consumption and discourages savings. An efficient tax system shouldn't distort the saving and consumption decision. This suggests implementing some type of consumption tax or reducing taxes on savings to level the playing field.

---

13. Banks subject to high corporation tax rates also find buying municipal bonds attractive.

PARABLE OF THE CAKERIES

Once upon a time, the Queen proclaimed, "Let them eat cake!"
To encourage the eating of cake, the Queen offered a 25-cent bounty for
every dollar of cake consumed. The idea for this came from her cousin,
Bartholomew, owner of the biggest cakery in the land. Cake sales
boomed, Cousin Bart smiled, and the peasantry gained weight. One
overweight loyal servant delightfully reported buying $4,000 in cakes and
receiving $1,000 in bounty at year's end. But the Queen's budget, which
had been balanced, went into deficit. The Crown was forced to borrow
money. The Queen's loyal adviser, the Captain of the Guards, was summoned. "What should be done?" she asked. "Taxes are high enough, your
Majesty, and subsidies are bad," he replied. "To avoid raising taxes, we
must eliminate the subsidy on cake." A royal decree ended the subsidy program, the Crown's budget returned to balance, the peasantry lost weight,
and the economy once again flourished.

• • •

Once upon a time, the Queen proclaimed, "Let them eat cake!"
To encourage the eating of cake, the Queen allowed all money spent on
cake consumption to be deducted from taxable income. The Kingdom's
tax rate was 25 percent, so every dollar spent on cake reduced taxes by
25 cents. The idea for this came from her shrewd cousin, Bartholomew,
owner of the biggest cakery in the land. Cake sales boomed, Cousin Bart
smiled and the peasantry gained weight. One overweight loyal servant
delightfully reported buying $4,000 in cakes and paying $1,000 less in
taxes than in the previous year despite earning the same income. "This
is great," he proclaimed. "It is exactly like getting a $1,000 subsidy to eat
cake!" But the Queen's budget, which had been balanced, went into deficit. The Crown was forced to borrow money. The Queen's loyal adviser,
the Captain of the Guards, was summoned. "What should be done?" she
asked. "Taxes are high enough, your Majesty, and eliminating the cake
deduction would raise the peasants' taxes." Gridlock in decision-making
occurred, deficits piled up, and the peasantry continued to gain weight.
The Crown went into bankruptcy, and the economy fell into disarray.

(Box continued on the next page)

The parables illustrate a well-known economic principle that tax deductions, also known as tax loopholes, are economically equivalent to explicit subsidy programs. The only significant difference is that loopholes hide the subsidies. In the first parable, the cake subsidy appears as an explicit outlay for the government; in the second parable, the subsidy is hidden and does not appear in the government's budget. While we may not subsidize cake purchases, U.S. tax laws subsidize such things as home purchases, the purchase of municipal bonds, and employer-provided health care. All told, our hidden subsidy programs total close to $1 *trillion* each year.

The Corporate Income Tax

At 35 percent, the maximum statutory U.S. corporate income tax rate is one of the highest in the world. Figure 5.2 provides some international comparisons of maximum statutory corporate tax rates imposed by federal governments. As in the case of individual income tax rates, corporate tax rates are graduated. Since the maximum U.S. rate applies to any corporate profits exceeding $335,000, the vast majority of corporate earnings are subject to the maximum rate. Interestingly, the capitalist United States has a higher maximum corporate income tax rate than communist China.

Most subnational governments in the United States also impose taxes on corporate income, just as they do on individuals' incomes. The average top corporate tax rate at the state level is 4 percent, making the combined top statutory rate slightly more than 39 percent. Within the group of countries that would include "old Europe," the United States, Canada, Australia, and Japan, the United States has the highest combined statutory corporate tax rate.[14]

Corporate Tax Expenditures: Subsidies for Corporations

Statutory tax rates are somewhat misleading as corporations also have their own tax loopholes—tax expenditures—providing subsidies that effectively lower the corporate tax burden. Like tax expenditures for the individual income

---

14. In 2012, Japan lowered its top rate.

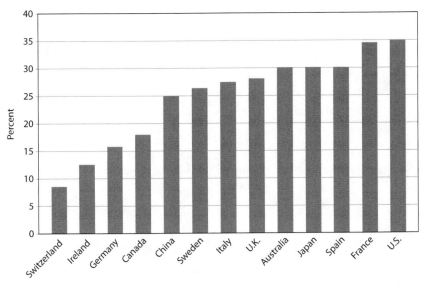

Source: OECD.

Figure 5.2. Maximum statutory corporate income tax rates, 2010.

tax, corporate tax expenditures also reduce the tax base, corporate income, in this case. Taking these corporate subsidies into account allows the computation of an "effective average tax rate." Although the U.S. makes more use of corporate tax expenditures than other countries on average, the effective U.S. average corporate tax rate of 29 percent is significantly higher than the 20.5 percent average for other developed countries.[15]

Corporate income taxes distort, and corporate tax expenditures distort further. One recent case of corporate subsidy was revealed in the subsidy for corporate jets. Congress and President Obama, seeking to spur economic growth, provided for an accelerated depreciation of new capital investments. Corporate jets, it turns out, are one such type of capital investment. The accelerated depreciation allows the corporation to deduct the cost of the jet faster than normal accounting practice allows, thereby reducing taxes sooner. Thus, corporations receive an extra tax subsidy to purchase a new corporate jet.

---

15. Kevin A. Hassett and Aparna Mathur, "Report Card on Effective Corporate Tax Rates," American Enterprise Institute, February 9, 2011. Retrieved from http://www.aei.org/outlook/101024.

Unfair Taxation and Multiple Taxation of Corporate Capital

Corporate profits, one type of business profit, are subject to the corporate income tax, but the taxation of these profits does not stop there. When corporations pay their shareholders dividends from their after-tax profits, the shareholders must declare the dividends as income and then pay the individual income tax on their dividends.[16] If corporations abstain from paying dividends, the retained profits boost the value of the company and their share prices rise, other things being equal. When the shareholder eventually sells the shares, the appreciated value of the stock is subject to capital gains taxation. So the owners of corporations pay corporate income taxes on their business income and then more taxes when cashing out of a company. This constitutes a multiple taxation of income on corporate capital. These high taxes on corporate capital encourage more financing with debt (borrowings) rather than using equity capital.

Consider two shareholders of XYZ stock, Joe with below-average wage income (and subject to the lowest marginal tax rate) and Joan with high wage income. Assume XYZ earns $10 per share before taxes and pays $3.20 per share in corporate income taxes. Both Joe and Joan, owners of XYZ, are implicitly paying the same 32 percent average tax rate on their income earned from XYZ. Joe, the low-income earner, pays the same tax rate as Joan, the high-income earner. This may lead Joe to decide that his savings are better invested in something like corporate bonds, where his interest income would be subject to his much lower marginal income tax rate. This makes corporate stock ownership, like municipal bonds, a poorer investment for lower income people. Is it fair that Joe pay the same tax rate on his corporate income as Joan? If you answer "yes," then why shouldn't Joe and Joan pay the same tax rate on their wage incomes?

Summing Up

Income taxes in the United States have been a primary source of tax revenues for nearly a hundred years. Over this time period, a relatively simple and transparent tax code has been replaced by a complex, nontransparent, and often unfair one that severely distorts economic decision-making. Like the weather, nearly everyone complains about our tax code, but no politician either can or

---

16. Some dividends qualify for the capital gains tax rather than the ordinary income tax.

cares to do anything constructive about it. The reason, in large part, is that the current tax code has served many politicians well. It has allowed for the dispensing of favors and hidden subsidies to friends and for the generation of lots of campaign contributions from special interest groups. But it has not served the country well.

Our national income, the sum of all wages, salaries, interest, rent, and profit, is now about $15 trillion per year. The federal budget for 2012 is expected to have outlays of about $3.7 trillion. If we wanted to balance the federal budget and maintain the current outlays, we could do so with a tax rate of 25 percent applied to *all* income. This would allow for elimination of Social Security and other federal payroll taxes, but it would not allow for any personal deductions or exemptions of any kind. Permitting exemptions or deductions would necessitate a higher tax rate, and adding a graduated tax-rate structure into the mix would push the highest marginal rates higher still. The higher these tax rates go, the more they distort and the more incentive special interests have to seek tax exemptions.

The United States is in a global competition with the rest of the world, and it participates in a global capital market where financial resources move freely. To remain competitive, taxation on capital must be competitive. Why not eliminate the corporate income tax? If we treat corporate profits as the personal income of the individual shareholders, each shareholder would be responsible for paying taxes based on the marginal tax rates deemed appropriate given his or her income level.

Measuring the economic waste associated with our income tax is complicated and has generated substantially different estimates by highly respected economists. One of the first estimates was made in 1964 by Arnold Harberger at the University of Chicago. He estimated economic losses at about 3 percent of revenue collected. For a $3 trillion annual federal budget, the annual economic loss would be about $90 billion. More recently in 1999, Martin Feldstein of Harvard University looked more broadly at the distortions caused by the income tax and concluded losses as high as 30 percent of revenue collected—ten times higher than the Harberger estimates. We can't answer here the question how large are the losses, but we can conclude that they are potentially very large. We can reduce much of these losses by having an income tax that distorts less. Lower marginal tax rates and the elimination of tax subsidies would achieve this.

There should be a way to rationalize the tax code, broaden the tax base, eliminate hidden subsidies, make the code transparent and fairer, and reduce marginal tax rates and their distorting effects. But how do we get there from here? Not easily. But with a sufficiently long phase-in period, the adjustments might be manageable. Unfortunately, the political forces and pressures that brought us our present tax code are still in play, and each special interest will strongly resist change. Each special interest will find political champions for their causes. All will make plausibly acceptable pleas for their needs and special considerations. Sadly, in such an environment, the prospect for serious change is unlikely.

Next up, the mother of all government Ponzi-type schemes: Medicare.

6

Medicare and Medicaid

Unsustainable Promises

> "It is my hope that many Republicans will join with the
> Democrats in voting for this very fine bill. It is a bill which is
> financially sound and which will benefit the entire nation."
> —*President Lyndon B. Johnson*, March 23, 1965

THE SOCIAL SECURITY Amendments of 1965, HR 6675, established the Medicare and Medicaid programs. President Lyndon Johnson signed the bill into law on July 30, 1965, in a ceremony held at the Harry S. Truman Presidential Library in Independence, Missouri. Truman, Johnson said, "planted the seeds of compassion and duty" that led to the Medicare program. Medicare established a federal heavily subsidized health care program for the elderly. Medicaid, another provision of the act, provided medical coverage including dental care to low-income individuals and families.[1] Contrary to President Johnson's claim, Medicare was anything but financially sound.

President Johnson did get some Republican support, but it was not needed. Democrats controlled more than two thirds of the votes in both the House and Senate, and HR 6675 would have passed without a single Republican vote. In the Senate, 57 of 64 Democrats supported the act; in the House, 237 of 307 Democrats voted in support. Although their support was not needed for passage, 13 Republican senators and 70 Republican representatives voted for the act. Most Republicans who cast votes in the House supported the act.

---

1. The costs of Medicaid, unlike Medicare, are shared by state governments and the federal government.

Figure 6.1. President Lyndon B. Johnson Signing the Medicare Bill, with
Lady Bird, Bess and Harry Truman and Vice President Humphrey.
Collection LBJ-WHPO: White House Photo Office Collection.

The act was a cornerstone in President Johnson's vision for the Great Society. It led to the greatest increase in nonmilitary government outlays since
Roosevelt's New Deal legislation, which established Social Security. In 2010,
Medicare and Medicaid (M&M) spent $793 billion, $92 billion more than Social Security. Although M&M outlays represented 22.9 percent of total federal
budget outlays, the current spending levels for M&M are just fender benders
compared to what's ahead. The big wreck coming results from the lack of tax
revenues to fund future promises. In the forecast, M&M's unfunded obligations are enormous, many times the magnitude of the shortfall for Social Security, one of our other follies. The present value of these unfunded obligations is
estimated to be about $36 trillion. This means that if we are to make good on
promises, given our current tax rates, we should have already accumulated $36
trillion in savings from which we could pay the future shortfall. To put this
into perspective, this amount is about 2.5 times our current national income
and substantially more than the value of all the shares on our nation's stock
exchanges.

Obviously, the massive tax deficiency requires that something will have to
give. While deficit spending might tide us over for a while, taxes will have to be
raised or costs decreased in the longer run. Unless some form of rationing of

medical services occurs, it is unlikely that much adjustment will come from decreases in costs. Most cost increases over time have been related to increasing sophistication in medical technology, a trend that is expected to continue. More likely, the size of government relative to the size of the economy will grow significantly, and this will require more taxes. Medicare has been structured and financed in a way that has reduced our national savings and shifted the responsibility for medical expenses in retirement from individuals and their families to taxpayers. Instead of accumulating private wealth to pay for retirement medical expenses, retirees now rely on public wealth, promises of payments based on the power of the federal government to tax. The increase in the size of government needed to keep the system going is likely to increase the normal unemployment rate and slow the growth of the economy. These issues will be discussed in detail in this chapter. With appropriately designed policies, this slow-motion wreck-in-the-making could have been avoided, but the short-run reelection goals of politicians would have been thwarted. Medicare and Medicaid is a well-deserved chapter in this book.

Social Safety Nets

Every nation wrestles with the issue of the social safety net. Should taxpayers guarantee minimum living standards for a nation's citizens? Should the impoverished be given an income guarantee? If so, how high should the guarantee be? The answers to these questions are subjective and depend on individual preferences concerning the society in which we wish to live. The specific choices society makes often produce highly different economic outcomes. Not only the distribution of income but also the economy's growth rate and future standard of living may be affected by our public policy decisions. Understanding all the implications of a public policy is important for making a sensible decision about its desirability, but, even knowing all the implications, we can still disagree on its desirability. We just may disagree about the kind of society we want or the importance of the future relative to the present.

Medicaid is a social safety net program targeted to help the lowest income individuals and families by improving their access to health care services. Most people support a Medicaid-type program, with disagreements focusing more on the details of the program rather than its general intent. Medicaid targets the poorest families among us and provides health care to their children, allowing them to have a better chance in life. The condition for receiving Medicaid benefits, serious financial hardship, is a condition most people would prefer to avoid if possible.

Medicare was established as a supplemental retirement program to provide heavily subsidized health insurance to people age 65 or older. Its recipients are, by and large, retirees who have worked over their lifetimes and have had economic opportunities and the ability to make major economic choices regarding savings and retirement. This makes Medicare much more problematic than Medicaid as a public policy.

The Politics of Medicare

The Social Security Act of 1935 strategically omitted any health care benefits. The Roosevelt Administration recognized that Social Security was contentious enough and feared that adding any public health insurance would kill the act. Thirty years later, Medicare and Medicaid were passed. Major advocates for the act were the labor unions and the Social Security Board, according to the reminiscences of then-Commissioner of Social Security Robert M. Ball.[2] Aligned against the act were the American Medical Association, most businesses, and the insurance industry.

Commissioner Ball recalls that supporters at the time saw Medicare as "a first step towards universal national health insurance," and they advocated its passage "solely because it seemed to have the best chance politically [as opposed to more sweeping legislation] . . . We wanted to get something going and this seemed a politically plausible first step." Public policies need to be plausibly acceptable to voters, and Commissioner Ball provides insight into the tactics used to make Medicare plausibly acceptable. The elderly, Commissioner Ball writes, were ill-suited for voluntary private coverage. Compared with younger people, they used on average more than twice as many hospital days and had half the income. Private insurers had to charge premiums to cover costs, and the elderly "could not afford the charges." Furthermore, "the need of the elderly

---

2. Robert M. Ball, "Perspectives on Medicare: What Medicare's Architects Had in Mind," *Health Affairs, 14*, no. 4, (1995), 62–72. Retrieved from http://content.healthaffairs.org/content/14/4/62.short.

was not hard to prove, nor was it difficult to prove that voluntary individual insurance was not only not [sic] meeting the need, but that it really could not."

Several problems exist with Commissioner Ball's statements. First, some private insurers offered health insurance for the elderly. It was indeed costly, just as auto insurance is costly for drivers with poor records. The elderly, even those who were affluent, no doubt were unhappy about the high premiums. So, many retirees who could afford health insurance chose not to purchase it. Second, the income of the elderly is clearly lower than those of younger members of society, but this is due in large part to their retirement status. Aside from income, however, retired people have an alternative way to pay for health insurance: out of private wealth. A 1960 University of Michigan Study investigating asset ownership by age groups found that a large majority of households headed by those age 65 or older had assets similar to the assets held by households headed by people age 45 to 64. Surely the majority of the elderly were able to pay for health insurance from private wealth, especially with Social Security providing income support. Medicare relieved even those who could afford private insurance from these expenses and allowed them to retire earlier and have greater use of their accumulated wealth for other types of spending or increased inheritance transfers.

Medicare converted the health care system for the elderly from a private, family responsibility to a societal responsibility. It could have been a system to subsidize only those with financial need, but instead it was extended to all elderly, regardless of need. Since payroll taxes are used to help fund Medicare payouts, when the program started, low-income workers helped to provide a free ride for many retirees, who were perfectly capable of paying for their own health care expenses. Transferring income from low-income low-wealth people to higher wealth people is a redistribution scheme that fails most definitions of fairness.

The payroll tax continues to give workers the illusion that they are saving for their future. These taxes are not saved; rather they are paid out to others on a pay-as-you-go basis, just like Social Security.

Pay-As-You-Go Systems

Medicare and Social Security are public programs to assist the elderly in retirement. They stand in sharp contrast to a purely private retirement system.

Consider Karen, planning for her retirement and knowing that no government assistance will be available. Karen will have to make decisions concerning savings, her desired retirement age, and her expected financial needs in retirement. Let's assume that Karen desires an early and comfortable retirement and saves diligently. In the absence of government assistance, she must accumulate enough savings to cover her retirement expenses. She invests in various assets during her working life: savings accounts, stocks, bonds, real estate, and maybe even some gold. While working, Karen purchases private health insurance and pays monthly premiums. Between saving and paying her insurance premiums, Karen often seems strapped for money and doesn't take too many vacations. Despite all this diligent saving and planning, things didn't quite work out as she expected. The premiums for health insurance post-retirement were much higher than she had planned, and some of her financial investments were a disappointment. As Karen approached her desired retirement age, she concluded that she had to work a few years longer to achieve her desired lifestyle in retirement.

The assets that Karen acquires are her private wealth. After retiring, Karen sells off her wealth assets, her private nest egg, to support her retirement expenses including health care-related costs. As Karen sells off her assets, the next generation of workers buys them as they save for their retirement. If the new generation desires an even better retirement lifestyle (or perhaps an even greater wealth transfer to their children) than Karen, it will save and invest even more than she did. Also, Karen's assets will contribute to the nation's wealth, and this wealth will grow over time if subsequent generations save more than the previous generation.

The wealth accumulation process determines the affluence of any nation. Some of Karen's savings go into loans that finance new plants and equipment, new commercial real estate, new start-up companies, and even loans to university students who raise the nation's human capital and production. With more physical and human capital and technology, workers become more productive, and wages rise. Wealth accumulation, capital formation, education, and technology combine to establish the prosperity of a nation. U.S. workers have at their disposal enormous amounts of physical and educational capital that help make their wages the envy of most of the world. Karen's and others' savings are crucially important in making this happen.

Medicare and Social Security also are retirement programs, but, unlike Karen's private retirement program, no private savings or wealth is accumulated to pay for future retirement needs.[3] The programs use pay-as-you-go financing (as noted in the Social Security chapter, this is a Ponzi-type scheme). Taxes are collected through a payroll tax, and these taxes are largely used to pay current benefits. Harry and Bess Truman received the first two Medicare cards, entitling them to medical benefits despite the fact that they had never paid any Medicare taxes. Early beneficiaries of Medicare, like those receiving the first Social Security checks, received many more dollars' worth of benefits above and beyond their tax contributions. Even retirees today are receiving many more benefits than their past contributions can justify—even if their tax contributions had been saved by the government for their retirement.

Eugene Steuerle and Stephanie Rennane[4] of the Urban Institute calculate that a couple earning average wages and retiring in 2011 can expect to receive $357,000 in medical benefits, although they contributed only $119,000 in payroll taxes including accrued interest.[5] If Medicare was run like Karen's private retirement fund, substantially more taxes should have been paid into the fund to justify the magnitude of the medical benefits. This, of course, would not have been very popular with taxpayer-voters, so, vote-maximizing politicians chose to "kick the can down the road," offering excessive benefits to the earliest retirees and letting future taxpayers bear the costs. Under a fully funded system with properly set tax rates, people retiring shortly after passage of Medicare, like Harry and Bess Truman, would have received little or no publicly provided benefits. Without these gifts to early beneficiaries, a large public nest egg would now exist. This public nest egg would have worked just like Karen's private retirement plan to raise the nation's wealth and productivity. But the public cupboard is bare because of our politicians' largesse. If a private retirement plan

---

3. Social Security and Medicare do have some accumulated "nest egg," but it is trivial compared to the fund that would exist under a Karen-type retirement plan.

4. C. Eugene Steuerle and Stephanie Rennane, "Social Security and Medicare Taxes and Benefits over a Lifetime," Urban Institute, June 2011. Retrieved from http://www.urban.org/UploadedPDF/social-security-medicare-benefits-over-lifetime.pdf.

5. Ricardo Alonso Zaldivar, "$114,000 That 2011 Retirees Paid into Medicare Won't Cover $355,000 in Lifetime Costs," Associated Press, December 30, 2010. Retrieved from http://www.cleveland.com/nation/index.ssf/2010/12/114000_that_2011_retirees_paid.html.

operated a pay-as-you-go system, its managers would be facing long prison terms like Bernie Madoff, a real Ponzi scheme pay-as-you-goer. In contrast, when politicians establish Ponzi-type schemes, they get reelected. Pay-as-you-go is a politician's dream: It immediately pays out enormous undeserved benefits to oh-so grateful voters and puts the costs on future generations.

Because future Medicare recipients are expecting the government—their public insurance company—to pay most of their future medical expenses, they need not accumulate as much private wealth as Karen to enjoy their retirement, and they are able to retire earlier than Karen. In essence, the government insurance leads people to substitute public wealth for private wealth. If Karen had qualified for Medicare, earned an average wage during her working life, remained single, and retired in 2011, Medicare would give Karen a gift of $128,000 in expected medical benefits in excess of her Medicare taxes (plus accrued interest). In other words, Karen could have saved $128,000 less privately during her working life, consuming more vacations and new cars or, perhaps, she could have retired earlier and still had the same expected lifestyle in retirement. Karen would have substituted some of her private wealth for her public wealth.

The big difference between private and public wealth is that private wealth has real assets behind it—assets that further economic growth and development. Public wealth has no real assets behind it, merely the promise to use the power of government to tax people in the future. Our pay-as-you-go systems have led to an increase in national consumption, earlier retirement decisions, and a decapitalization in society—a loss of productive assets. If our pay-as-you-go Medicare and Social Security had been fully funded, we would now have trillions of dollars invested in China, not the reverse.[6] How did all this happen? Politicians suffering from immediosis (see Introduction) just did politician things. They couldn't keep their hands out of the cookie jar. They provided and continue to provide unwarranted medical benefits to current retired voters and kick the burden of taxation down the road to future voters and future politicians. They merely follow the Golden Rule of politics: provide benefits now, costs later.

---

6. U.S. "sovereign wealth"—the nest egg accumulated by government—would be many trillions of dollars.

Excess Promises

Most Americans retiring today have paid into Medicare all their lives and feel they are entitled to their health care benefits. Aside from the fact that their Medicare payroll taxes have already been given away, when we look at the benefits versus the taxes paid, enormous subsidies are still being given. Medicare, just like Social Security, is a political "third rail." Stepping on the third rail of the electric train track ensures electrocution. Similarly, stepping on Medicare by suggesting a reduction in benefits is political suicide.

This is understandable. Medicare gave the retirees the promise of public wealth, and as a result, more private consumption took place during their working lives. Seniors are less able to pay for their own retirement expenses as a result. But the truth is that, given promised benefits to retirees, much more should have been collected in taxes over their working lives—an amount so large as to frighten almost everyone.

Let's look at a two-earner couple in 2011. One earns an above-average wage of $69,600 and the other an average wage of $43,500. If they began work at age 22 (and one earned an above-average and the other an average salary) and started to collect Medicare benefits at age 65 in 2011, they can expect to receive $357,000 in Medicare benefits. Their Medicare taxes, including accumulated interest on what they paid in to the system, amount to only $149,000. Under a purely private retirement system, this couple would have had to save nearly $200,000 more in their lifetime above-and-beyond Medicare payroll taxes to pay for their expected medical costs in retirement.

Next, consider the two-earner couple, one with an average wage and the other earning 45 percent of an average wage. This couple earns $63,000 in 2011. Retiring in 2011, their expected Medicare benefits in excess of their contributions are $271,000. This means aside from their other savings for retirement, this couple would have had to save an additional $271,000 for the same lifestyle and medical benefits in retirement.

These examples point out the enormous costs of post-retirement health care. Private insurance companies offering health insurance coverage for the elderly need to cover these costs, and the insurance premiums need to be correspondingly large. If these retirement costs were to be covered by the retirees themselves, they would need a substantial nest egg or delay retirement. But since they have a Medicare guarantee that provides a substantial subsidy (above and beyond what had already been paid in payroll taxes), they retire without the requisite savings. Worse yet, since their payroll taxes have not been saved for their retirement medical costs, the next generation of taxpayers must bear the full costs.

Medicare Part D

The Medicare Prescription Drug, Improvement, and Modernization Act of 2003 (MPDA) provides a recent case study in political entrepreneurship, political myopia, and the role of money in policy-making, all combining to produce a wreck within a wreck. MPDA was the largest entitlement program to be enacted in more than forty years, initially estimated to cost $400 billion over the first ten years. The act established, among other things, Medicare Part D, a new program to subsidize medicinal drugs for the elderly. Democrats, who have long championed subsidies to the elderly and those in need (for example, Social Security, Medicare, and Medicaid), had identified a new hardship for the elderly: financial strain caused by rapidly rising drug prices. In 2003, Republicans held the White House, and George W. Bush seized the initiative. "Our nation has made a promise, a solemn promise, to America's seniors," Bush said. "We have pledged to help our citizens find affordable medical care in the later years of life . . . These reforms are the act of a vibrant and compassionate government," he said.[7]

It is merely conjecture, but President Bush also may have been mindful of the political importance of seniors, a group well-known for its high turnout at the polls. In any event, seniors age 65 and above increased their support for President Bush. In 2004, 52 percent supported Bush, up from 47 percent in 2000.

In Congress, the vote for MPDA split strongly along party lines, and the act almost failed in the House, passing by a mere two-vote margin. In the House, Republicans, many of them strong-armed into support, favored the act 207 to

---

7. "Bush Signs Landmark Medicare Bill Into Law," CNN, December 8, 2003. Retrieved from http://articles.cnn.com/2003-12-08/politics/elec04.medicare_1_prescription-drug-private-insurers-medicare?_s=pm:allpolitics.

19; Democrats voted against 195 to 9. In the Senate, more than 75 percent of the Democrats voted against while more than 80 percent of the Republicans voted support. Democrats, hardly ever missing an opportunity to support welfare transfers, uncharacteristically rejected the act. Democrats claimed they were particularly angered by what they perceived to be a big giveaway to pharmaceutical interests that might undermine the entire Medicare program with cost overruns. An important factor is that the act explicitly prohibited the government from negotiating drug prices with pharmaceutical companies.[8] The Department of Veterans Affairs, in contrast, negotiates drug prices and pays considerably less for drugs than Medicare Part D. The act guaranteed the drug companies a free hand in the pricing of their drugs and a tidy increase in profits. Democrats also may have been miffed by the gall of a Republican president taking the initiative in a traditionally Democrat arena.

Representative Billy Tauzin (R-LA), chair of the Energy and Commerce Committee and a principal author of the act, played an important role in keeping it pharmaceutically friendly. In 2004, one year after passage of the act, Tauzin was appointed president of the drug industry trade group, Pharmaceutical Research and Manufacturers of America (known commonly as PhRMA), his reported salary somewhere between $2 million and $2.5 million a year.

More shenanigans concerning passage of the legislation surrounds Thomas A. Scully, administrator of the Centers for Medicare and Medicaid Services from 2001 to 2003. Scully acknowledged that he suppressed a cost estimate for Medicare D that was some 50 percent higher than the Bush administration's original estimate. This new figure might have swayed some members of the House to withdraw support for the act, and it would have died. While the legislation was being debated, Scully was hard at work negotiating a job with a Washington law office, where he would become a pharmaceutical lobbyist, a mere fifteen days after the act was passed.[9]

---

8. Robert Peark, "House's Author of Drug Benefit Joins Lobbyists," *New York Times,* December 16, 2004. Retrieved from http://www.nytimes.com/2004/12/16/politics/16drug.html?_r=1&ref=billytauzin.

9. Michelle Singer, "Under the Influence," *60 Minutes,* February 11, 2009, Retrieved from http://www.cbsnews.com/stories/2007/03/29/60minutes/main2625305_page3.shtml?tag=contentMain; contentBody.

Medicare Part D provides seniors with a new source of public wealth, a wealth claim that allows them to save less privately during their working lives because most of their drug needs now are taken care of in retirement. Part D provided a new lucrative business for the pharmaceutical industry, created campaign donations and jobs for supporters of the act, and garnered more senior citizens' votes for an incumbent president seeking reelection. It left taxpayers with a bill that continues to grow.

Growth in Entitlements and the Growth in Government

The predicted growth in our various entitlement programs as a percentage of our national income represents one of the greatest challenges facing the economy. In 2010, federal spending on Social Security, Medicare, and Medicaid consumed about 10 percent of our national income, and the share is expected to reach 20 percent by 2054. Figure 6.2 shows that Medicare's share over this period is expected to surge from 3.5 percent of national income to almost 10 percent. Medicaid's share of national income will rise as well, but Social Security outlays as a percentage of national income are expected to remain fairly constant. These estimates are likely to be underestimates as they were made before passage of President Obama's Affordable Care Act, which substantially expands coverage for Medicaid and provides subsidies for workers to buy health insurance.

Some Effects of Big Governments

Recent research has investigated the effects of government size on economic growth and the economy's normal unemployment rate. The findings are fairly consistent that countries with larger governments, measured as a bigger share of the total economy, tend to have lower economic growth rates and higher unemployment rates. Bergh and Karlsson, writing in the journal *Public Choice* in 2010, find statistical evidence using international comparisons that big governments reduce economic growth. Ghosh Roy, using U.S. data, reports in a study published in the journal *Applied Economics* in 2009 that larger government size reduces U.S. growth. Afonso and Furceri in the *European Journal of Political Economy* in 2010 support the findings of Bergh and Karlsson.

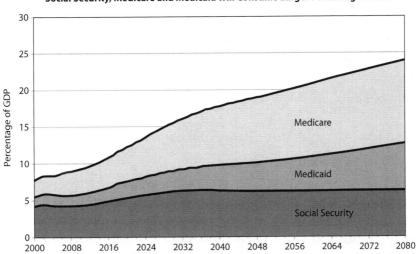

Social Security, Medicare and Medicaid Will Consume Larger Percentage of GDP

Source: Government Accounting Office, U.S. Financial Condition and
Fiscal Future Briefing, January 2008.

Figure 6.2. Predicted GDP share for entitlements.

Bigger governments also are associated with higher unemployment rates, and the evidence is that bigger governments cause the higher unemployment and not the reverse. These studies complement the growth studies. If bigger governments reduce economic growth, it isn't surprising that unemployment rates are higher. Unemployed people in slower growing economies can be expected to have more difficulty finding a job than unemployed in faster growing economies. Christopoulos and others writing in *Applied Economics* in 2005, using data on ten European countries, find support for the government size-unemployment rate linkage. Feldmann reports in *Applied Economics Letters* in 2010, using data from 52 developing countries, that bigger governments increase unemployment rates. My own research with colleague Siyan Wang using data from all developed countries adds support to the ideas that bigger governments slow growth and raise the unemployment rate.

Why do bigger governments seem to generate these negative economic effects? It is not obvious that they should. Certainly bigger governments could spend monies in ways that further economic growth and employment. Spending on infrastructure, education, and basic research are known to be growth enhancing. Yet, many other programs can be wasteful and counterproductive, such as pay-as-you-go programs that decapitalize economies. As another example, consider the soil conservation program that gave subsidies to farmers to leave their fields unplanted. Furthermore, overly generous welfare systems and unemployment compensation programs can encourage some people to avoid seriously searching for employment. Big governments must have big taxes, and taxes themselves can be counterproductive in job creation.

Comparing the United States with Europe helps to illustrate an explanation for the statistical findings. On average, Western European governments are considerably bigger, spending a larger share of their national incomes, than the United States. Their social safety nets are more generous than those found in the United States. Almost all provide universal health care and unemployment insurance, which often lasts longer and replaces more of the unemployed person's lost income. European taxes are much higher and their discretionary incomes much lower. On average, Western European countries grow more slowly; they have significantly lower per capita real incomes—about 30 percent lower than in the United States—and higher "normal" unemployment rates than the United States. Their lagging economic performance compared to the United States has been given a name—*Eurosclerosis*, a hardening of the economic arteries. The evidence suggests that big governments in Western Europe tax and spend monies in many ways that are simply not conducive to economic growth.

Certainly, this does not mean European governments are "bad." Again, it just depends on what type of society one prefers. Europeans have less poverty, more vacation time, and retire earlier. For many, this is quite desirable. But these benefits come with economic costs: lower growth, lower incomes, and higher unemployment rates. Are Americans prepared to bear these costs?

Patient Protection and Affordable Care Act (PPACA)

PPACA was signed into law by President Barack Obama in 2010. Most major provisions of the act will be phased in by January 2014. The effect of the act on medical costs and the changes in tax rates that might be needed to finance the program have been subject of numerous studies, but no real consensus has developed as of 2012. The act greatly expands the Medicaid program by allowing people with higher income levels to qualify. The act also calls for major subsidies to families not receiving employer-provided health insurance to assist their purchases of health care insurance. These subsidies will be given to many families well above the poverty level.[10] For example, the Kaiser Family Foundation estimates that a family of four headed by a person age 50 and earning $90,000 will receive more than $8,000 in cashable tax credits.[11] How the act impacts work incentives, the unemployment rate, economic growth, and the tax burden of government may provide material for a chapter in the next book on economic blunders.

Summing Up

Medicare is a pay-as-you-go system. Payroll taxes are not saved and invested as would have been the case if individuals and their families were responsible for their health care costs in retirement. The program was overly generous to early retirees and continues to provide extraordinary payouts to even average wage earners retiring today. The system has encouraged a substitution of public wealth for private wealth that has increased our national consumption and lowered the accumulation of real wealth in society. As a result, Medicare is responsible for decapitalizing the United States. By how much? The amount is likely to be in the trillions of dollars. Some of this decapitalization has been offset by foreign capital inflows. The United States has been selling off its wealth assets to foreigners. While we still have much the same total plant and equipment, much more of it is now foreign owned. As a result, a larger share of U.S.-generated profits and interest on bonds goes to foreigners, not U.S. citizens. Our lack of savings as a nation has made us poorer.

Our publicly provided health care programs are expected to consume an ever-increasing percentage of our national income going forward. The Office of Management and Budget's estimate is that Medicare and Medicaid would raise outlays as a percentage of national income by 10 percentage points by 2054. Let's assume that military outlays are reduced and health care cost savings are able to hold the growth in the size of the federal government to 5 percent of

---

10. Subsidies are already given to people who receive employer-provided health care insurance. See Ch 1.

11. For a website to compute expected subsidies to families with different incomes and age characteristics see: http://healthreform.kff.org/SubsidyCalculator.aspx#incomeAgeTables.

national income. This would increase the size of government from roughly 20 percent to 25 percent of national income. Many economic studies suggest that this government growth will lower U.S. economic growth and raise its normal unemployment rate. A statistical study done with colleague Siyan Wang suggests that a 5 percent increase in the share of the economy going to the federal budget would raise the normal U.S. unemployment rate by 2.8 percentage points.[12] If the normal unemployment rate was 5 percent, the new normal rate would be 7.8 percent. This would put the United States close to the Western European average unemployment rate.

The wreck in all this is that the negative effects of Medicare on wealth, growth, and the unemployment rate were all avoidable. The government could have established a publicly run, fully funded system. A U.S. sovereign wealth fund, real wealth overseen by the government or private agents, could have established a nest egg to meet future outlays. The fund would be drawn down to meet medical costs for retirees, but the next generation would replenish it with their taxes. Such a system could have been devised that still provided subsidies to those most in need. But such a system would have violated the politicians' golden rule to provide immediate benefits and to forestall taxes. Politicians provided some individuals with a free lunch, but the bill is now being delivered.

The next chapter provides concrete evidence of political immediosis and its high cost. It is the story of Richard Nixon and his manipulation of the economy to win reelection.

---

12. Burton A. Abrams and Siyan Wang, "The Effect of Government Size on the Steady-State Unemployment Rate: A Structural Error Correction Model" (Working Paper 2006–05), University of Delaware, Department of Economics, 2006. Retrieved from http://www.lerner.udel.edu/economics/WorkingPapers/2006/UDWP2006-05.pdf.

7

The Nixon-Burns
Political Business Cycle[1]
How to Create a Decade of Inflation

"I've never seen anybody beaten on inflation in the United States. I've seen many people beaten on unemployment."
—*President Richard Nixon*, from a secretly recorded White House tape

THE 1970S WAS the decade of inflation, the worst U.S. inflation in over one hundred years. On average, an item that cost one dollar in 1970 cost over two dollars in 1980. In the last year of the decade, prices for consumer goods increased 14 percent. Three presidents fought heroic battles against inflation throughout the decade, or so it seemed.

In 1971, President Richard Nixon took the dramatic action of imposing wage and price controls. But after the controls were lifted, inflation worsened. In 1974, President Gerald Ford introduced a program to Whip Inflation Now that spawned WIN buttons. As one spin-off to the program, the White House planted a WIN garden and encouraged Americans to do the same. Presumably the increased supply of agricultural products would hold down food prices and inflation. Not surprisingly, the WIN campaign failed to stop the inflation.

In a 1978 televised address to the nation, President Jimmy Carter told a troubled nation:

---

1. Much of this chapter draws from Burton A. Abrams, "How Richard Nixon Pressured Arthur Burns: Evidence from the Nixon Tapes," *Journal of Economic Perspectives* 20(4), 2006, and Burton A. Abrams and James L. Butkiewicz, "The Political Business Cycle: New Evidence from the Nixon Tapes," *Journal of Money, Credit and Banking*, 44, nos. 2–3 (March 2012): 385–99.

Inflation is obviously a serious problem. What is the solution? I do not have all the answers. Nobody does. Perhaps there is no complete and adequate answer. But I want to let you know that fighting inflation will be a central preoccupation of mine during the months ahead, and I want to arouse the nation to join me in this effort.[2]

Some economists, otherwise seemingly sensible, searching for innovative ways to tame inflation recommended TIPS, tax-incentive policies that would tax firms that raised prices in excess of the government's guidelines and provide subsidies to those that raised prices less than the guidelines. Never mind the enormous economic distortions and bureaucratic costs such a program would produce. The policy rewarded old products— say an eight-track tape player— where falling prices reflected the fact that few people still wanted them. Its producers would receive a subsidy. Conversely, new products—where rising prices reflected short supply—would be punished with a tax. This wastes resources by encouraging the production of undesired goods while discouraging the production of desired goods. Fortunately, TIPS never flew.

Inflation had to be stopped. During the 1970s, the *misery index* proved popular with the public and media. Add the inflation rate to the unemployment rate to obtain the misery index. Notably, the inflation rate was given equal weight to the unemployment rate in computing macroeconomic misery. In presidential elections, challengers made good use of the misery index. Jimmy Carter pointed out how the misery index had risen under President Ford's watch. And Ronald Reagan used the same argument against President Carter. The point is that inflation was politically unpopular, and during the 1970s, only one president was able to get reelected: President Nixon, who managed to reduce the misery index in the 1972 election year in large part by imposing wage and price controls (see Figure 7.1).

Yet, in August 1979, the inflation rate was still surging at 14 percent. President Carter asked the head of the Federal Reserve Bank, G. William Miller, to step in as Treasury Secretary. A lawyer by training and previous CEO of Textron, Miller noted that his purpose in moving to Treasury was to make a bigger impact on the fight against inflation. Never mind that the power to

---

2. October 24, 1978. http://www.pbs.org/wgbh/americanexperience/features/primary-resources/carter-anti-inflation/.

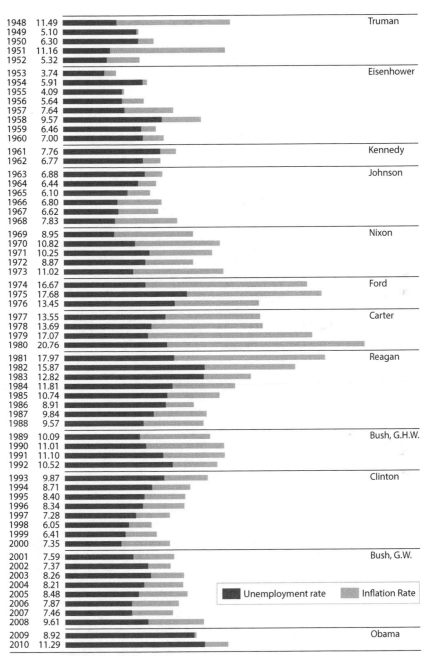

1948	11.49		Truman
1949	5.10		
1950	6.30		
1951	11.16		
1952	5.32		
1953	3.74		Eisenhower
1954	5.91		
1955	4.09		
1956	5.64		
1957	7.64		
1958	9.57		
1959	6.46		
1960	7.00		
1961	7.76		Kennedy
1962	6.77		
1963	6.88		Johnson
1964	6.44		
1965	6.10		
1966	6.80		
1967	6.62		
1968	7.83		
1969	8.95		Nixon
1970	10.82		
1971	10.25		
1972	8.87		
1973	11.02		
1974	16.67		Ford
1975	17.68		
1976	13.45		
1977	13.55		Carter
1978	13.69		
1979	17.07		
1980	20.76		
1981	17.97		Reagan
1982	15.87		
1983	12.82		
1984	11.81		
1985	10.74		
1986	8.91		
1987	9.84		
1988	9.57		
1989	10.09		Bush, G.H.W.
1990	11.01		
1991	11.10		
1992	10.52		
1993	9.87		Clinton
1994	8.71		
1995	8.40		
1996	8.34		
1997	7.28		
1998	6.05		
1999	6.41		
2000	7.35		
2001	7.59		Bush, G.W.
2002	7.37		
2003	8.26		
2004	8.21		
2005	8.48	Unemployment rate Inflation Rate	
2006	7.87		
2007	7.46		
2008	9.61		
2009	8.92		Obama
2010	11.29		

Source: NPA Services, Inc. The Unemployment Rate figures obtained from the U.S. Department of Labor, www.dol.gov. The Inflation Rate figures obtained from Financial Trend Forecaster®, www.InflationData.com. Reprinted by permission.

Figure 7.1. The Misery Index

control the money printing press and inflation resides with the Fed, not the Treasury. Ironically, Miller was correct. His move to Treasury provided a key ingredient in the fight against inflation: the installation of a new chair of the Fed, someone who knew how to whip inflation, economist Paul Volcker.

Volcker took the old-fashioned approach to fighting inflation: He stopped the Fed's money printing press. Interest rates soared. The federal funds rate, the interest rate that banks charge when lending to each other overnight, peaked at more than 22 percent. The economy entered two back-to-back recessions and, during one stretch that lasted almost a year, the unemployment rate rose to more than 10 percent. Inflation's back finally was broken, but the economic cost to the country was enormous.

Many culprits have been identified to explain the inflation of the 1970s. Heading the list were the Organization of Petroleum-Exporting Countries and its oil price increases, out-of-control unions demanding higher wages that pushed prices higher, and the public's unjustified inflationary expectations. But now the Nixon tapes reveal that the real culprit was the government itself. A master of political maneuvering, Nixon engineered a speed-up in the money printing press to produce an economic upswing to coincide with his 1972 re-election bid. He did this despite numerous warnings that such a policy would worsen an already bad inflation. To further his political goals, he put the econ-

Figure 7.2. Arthur Burns, John Connally, Richard M. Nixon, Paul McCracken, and George Shultz. Photo by Oliver F. Atkins, 1916-1977, Photographer, (NARA record: 8451334).

omy on an inflationary course that could be reversed only at enormous cost to the nation in the longer run. The story of Nixon's shortsighted policy decisions purely designed to benefit his reelection is a worthy chapter in the line-up of worst economic policies of the past hundred years. The episode highlights why it is vital to keep the power of the money printing press out of the reach of politicians.

Economic Conditions and Presidential Elections

Everybody probably remembers Bill Clinton's famous 1992 slogan, "It's the economy, stupid." But long before 1992, economists discovered the importance of favorable economic conditions for incumbent presidents and their parties. This was not lost on Nixon, who had blamed his narrow defeat in the 1960 presidential election on a sluggish economy.

Early in 1960, on the advice of economist Arthur Burns, Vice President Nixon approached President Dwight Eisenhower to seek his help in pressuring the Fed to speed up the printing press and asking the Congress to pass tax cuts or increases in defense spending to get the economy moving. Eisenhower said he would do no such thing unless recession warranted it. Nixon did not get the boost to the economy he desired, and he lost a close election. It was a lesson he would not forget.

Since favorable economic conditions boost a president's reelection chances, we should not be surprised to find presidents seeking policies designed to boost the economy and lower unemployment in the run-up to the election. Expansionary monetary policy cranks up the money printing press. The creation of new money causes interest rates to fall, at least in the short run, and gives banks new funds to lend. Expansionary fiscal policies consist of cutting taxes, increasing transfer payments such as Social Security payouts, and increasing government spending. Both expansionary monetary and fiscal policies are thought to increase spending and employment in the economy, at least for some time. Timing is everything.

Economists observe delays, or lags, in the effectiveness of these policies, pointing out that "the lags are long and variable." So, presidents who want to window-dress the economy by election time should start the expansionary monetary or fiscal policy well before the election—and hope for the best. Too late and there will be no effect in time for the election; too early and the hoped-for effect may peter out too soon.

The idea that presidents might engage in such manipulations of the economy for political gain has spawned the idea of a *political business cycle*. Evidence for a political business cycle would be a boom-bust cycle coinciding with presidential election dates: booms in the run-up to elections and slowdowns after the election, caused by reversals in monetary and fiscal policies to prevent the inflationary consequences of the pre-election boom. In studying the data, economists find mixed evidence. Clearly, unanticipated lags in the effects of monetary and fiscal policies may hide attempts at manipulating the economy, and certainly not all presidents succumb to the temptations of manipulating the economy. Furthermore, it's hard to prove the underlying motive for a president's policies, which is why the Nixon tapes provide such a valuable resource. Beginning in February 1971, Richard Nixon secretly began taping conversations that took place in the White House. The tapes now give irrefutable evidence that Nixon deliberately engineered a business cycle for political gain. It would be hard to believe that he was or will be the only president to do so.

Nixon and Arthur Burns

In 1969, President Richard Nixon nominated Arthur F. Burns as the chairman of the Federal Reserve, and Burns took office on February 1, 1970. Burns was a respected economist with years of experience and impressive credentials: professor of economics at Columbia University, president of the National Bureau of Economic Research from 1957 to 1967, and chairman of the Council of Economic Advisors under President Eisenhower from 1953 to 1957. He was an authority on business cycles and monetary policy and published extensively.

Although Burns was an eminent economist, Nixon was probably more impressed with the fact that he was a sympathetic Republican loyalist. Burns had recommended that Nixon seek Eisenhower's aid in boosting the economy in 1960. Although Eisenhower refused, Nixon knew that Burns had called it right and demonstrated that he had Nixon's political interests at heart.

When Burns took command of the Fed in 1970, the economy was in an inflationary recession, or *stagflation*. The options facing Burns and the Fed were either to hold tight controls on the money printing press to fight the inflation while risking a deepening in the recession or to speed up the money printing press to stimulate employment growth while risking a worsening in the inflation rate. Nixon preferred the latter, and the evidence shows that Burns gave Nixon what he wanted.

By February 1971, Burns had overseen a full year of a faster money printing press, but Nixon wanted even more. Burns resisted. The following quotes are from Nixon's secretly taped conversations in the White House.

Burns (to Nixon): "In my view the monetary authority . . . has laid the foundation for recovery. . . . What is holding back the economy now is not any shortage of money but a certain shortage of confidence. If we flooded the banks even more than we have I think you could have awful problems in 1972 and beyond."

Burns clearly states that he has already flooded the banks with money. He worries that cranking up the printing press more will cause inflation in 1972 and beyond.

In March 5, 1971, Treasury Secretary John Connally joined Nixon in exhorting Burns to flood the banks with even more money, but again Burns resisted.

Connally: "We need to drive this interest rate down."

Burns: "We could make matters worse by making money easier . . . If anybody gets the notion, you see, that we are easing monetary policy further, that will intensify these fears of a rise in interest rates later on."

Burns again clearly indicated that he had, in his view, done enough pumping up of the money supply. Burns fully understood that too much money now meant worsening inflation down the road and a reversal of policy later. Both would drive interest rates up later on. At the end of the meeting, Connally stayed to talk with Nixon, who praised his Treasury Secretary for stressing the need to lower interest rates. Both Nixon and Connally were beginning to view Burns as the enemy. They wanted and needed Burns to cooperate.

Nixon: "He's [Burns is] ruthless. He plays all the bureaucracy. He plays all the press. He does the leaks. He does everything else, John."

Connally: "He plays that Hill . . . in a big way. Both sides."

Nixon: "I'd be delighted to be the first President in 25 years to take the Fed on if it becomes necessary."

Connally: "He can force these interest rates down and that ought to be done."

Nixon was clearly frustrated by Burns's independence and indicated he was prepared to "take on" the Fed to get his desired monetary policy, and he began to lay his plans.

Eleven days later, on March 16, 1971, Nixon and Connally discussed the need to control Burns and how to do it. Connally said he would talk to Burns and tell him to stay out of Connally's territory. He would tell Burns, "If you want to maintain the independence of this Federal Reserve System, you oughtn't to be talking about wage and price policies and fiscal affairs . . . it's not your business . . . sure you're knowledgeable about it, but what the hell, you're running the Federal Reserve now."

The threat to Burns was clear: You mess in our business, we'll be forced to mess in yours. The Fed was created in 1913 and given substantial independence to prevent political manipulations, but Nixon and Connally now plotted to undermine the independence of the Fed for political gain. This was the first mention in the Nixon tapes concerning an explicit threat to the independence of the Fed. There were more.

Nixon and Connally continue.

Nixon: "He is also wrong in terms of monetary supply, damn it! Everybody except Arthur thinks it [the money supply] ought to be higher and let's just keep hitting him on that . . . He [Burns] must not do things that are going to embarrass the Administration."

Contrary to Nixon's claim that "everybody" thought the money supply should be higher, Milton Friedman, the preeminent authority on monetary policy, told Nixon in two separate taped conversations that monetary policy was already too expansionary. Nixon ignored Friedman's advice.

In a subsequent conversation with Burns, Nixon laid down his cards.

Nixon (to Burns): "We've really got to think of goosing it . . . late summer and fall of this year [1971] and next year [1972]. As you know there's a hell of a lag."

Two days later, Connally reported to the president about his meeting with Burns. Connally's message to Burns was that Burns was losing his influence in the Administration. Connally reported that he told Burns, "You're isolating yourself more and more. . . . Normally the Treasury and Federal Reserve will be right together and that's the way I want it, but if you're going to isolate yourself, I can't go with you.'"

Connally and Nixon were letting Burns know that he was rapidly becoming the odd-man out due to his opposition to flooding the banks even more. By being too independent, Burns was told, he was isolating himself. Burns needed to get onboard with the administration or face the consequences.

The next day, March 19, Nixon and Burns met. Burns was upset about criticism through press leaks. He emphasized his loyalty to the president.

> **Burns [to the President]:** "I'm doing my basic job at the Fed [tape skips] I'm a dedicated man, to serve the health and strength of our national economy, and I've done everything in my power, as I see it to help keep pressing your reputation, your standing in American life and in history. I've never seen a conflict between the two. But I want you to know this, if a conflict did arise, the moment a conflict arises, I'm going to be right here [Burns bangs the table for emphasis]. And I'll tell you about it and we'll talk it out, and try to decide together where to go next."

Burns wanted Nixon to know he was still a loyal soldier and that compromise was possible. But Burns made it clear he still believed his monetary policy shouldn't be changed:

> **Burns:** "To drive interest rates lower would run the risk of accelerating an international monetary crisis."

Burns knew that lower interest rates would accelerate the flight from the dollar as investors would seek higher rates in other countries. In addition, foreign holders of dollars would convert their dollars into gold and accelerate gold withdrawals from the United States. At the time, the United States was running dangerously low on gold reserves. Burns worried that the cupboard would soon be bare.

Burns raised yet another justification for his resistance to easing monetary policy. He warned that lowering interest rates now (March 19, 1971) would cause rates to increase during the election year, with the implication that the resulting damage to housing would hurt Nixon's reelection chances.

Burns: "If interest rates go down further through my actions . . . the probability as I see it is, they will go up later on in the year and in 1972. Housing which is recovering very nicely will go into a tailspin in 1972. Where will we be, as a country, and as a party and me personally?"

Again, Burns emphasized the adverse longer run effects on inflation and interest rates if the Fed further flooded the banks with money.

On June 8, 1971, Milton Friedman visited the White House. He warned Nixon against using the money printing press to try to reduce interest rates or unemployment. He feared the printing press was already running too quickly and that a revival in inflation would make the previous recession for naught. Since inflation is the consequence of speeding up the money printing press, slowing down the printing press is usually the cure. Unfortunately, slowing down the printing press tends to cause recessions, a negative effect of slowing down the printing press that seems to be unavoidable. The United States suffered from rising inflation in the late 1960s and Nixon was elected to the presidency in a recession caused by a slow-down in the printing press. Gains had been made in the fight against inflation, but now Friedman worried that the gains would be lost because the printing press once again had been speeded up.

Friedman: I'm not optimistic because you cannot avoid a rise in interest rates in the next six months . . . I don't know a thing about politics. But it does seem to me that nothing could be more damaging to you in 1972 . . . [than] if the price rise in 1972 is back up to 7%. I think in general unemployment is much more damaging politically than inflation. . . . but in the particular case of your administration and yourself it [inflation] is even [tape skips] because we took extra measures to do something about it [inflation]. And now it must pay off.

Friedman's advice about the political costs of reviving inflation had no impact on Nixon, whose primary concern was reducing unemployment. In July 1971, one month after the Friedman visit, Nixon clearly revealed his interest in the unemployment rate and indifference to inflation. Speaking of the impact of economic factors on election outcomes, he told Peter Peterson, assistant to the president for international economic affairs: "I've never seen anybody beaten on inflation in the United States. I've seen many people beaten on unemployment."

Also in July 1971, Nixon and George Shultz, director of the Office of Management and Budget, discussed a possible vacancy on the Federal Reserve Board. Nixon, wanting to increase the pressure on Burns, told Shultz to inform Burns that he already had someone in mind for the position, although in fact he had not identified a candidate.

> **Nixon:** "I'll tell you what I've done. I've told Connally to find the easiest money man[3] he can find in the country. And one that will do exactly what Connally wants and one that will speak up to Burns . . . and Connally is searching the god damn hills of Texas, California, Ohio. We'll get a populist senator [sic] on that Board one way or another. . . . If you know of someone that's that crazy let me know too . . . I want a man on that Board that I can control. I really do. Basically that Connally can control . . . But Arthur's not going to name that man to the Board, George."

The seven members of the Board of Governors are each appointed by the president to serve fourteen-year terms. Long terms presumably allow governors to put short-run political considerations aside when voting on monetary policy. Nixon's scheme to appoint a reduce-unemployment-at-all-cost governor demonstrates one way that presidential immediosis (short-run bias) can be injected into Fed policymaking.

To further pressure Burns, Nixon told his close advisers, John Ehrlichman and H. R. Haldeman, to leak a story through Charles Colson, special counsel to the president, about a recommendation to expand the Federal Reserve Board.

> **Nixon:** "Could you get one story leaked through the Colson apparatus about Arthur? . . . Recommendations are being made from among the President's economic advisors that . . . recommended that the Federal Reserve Board . . . the membership be expanded."

Expanding the seven-member board would weaken Burns's powers, especially if the additional appointees were loyal to Nixon, who also wanted another rumor leaked.

---

3. An "easy money man" is someone who would let the money printing press roll faster.

Nixon: "In view of the fact that the President has responsibility for full employment, the president is considering legislation to . . . the Fed has got to be brought in the—"

Haldeman: "—in the executive branch."

Nixon: "The independence of the Fed—"

Haldeman: "—is seriously in question."

Nixon: "Connally feels, John and Bob, that it'd be helpful . . . he thinks it might sort of worry Arthur a little."

While the Fed is a quasi-private organization, its powers are derived from federal legislation. Laws can be changed, and Nixon now spread rumors that he might do so in a way that would reduce the independence of the Fed.

Nixon and Haldeman continued discussing two pending vacancies on the Federal Reserve Board and the bias Nixon intended to introduce into the Fed's policy decisions.

Nixon: "We're going to fill 'em both with basically easy money men."

Haldeman: "George [Shultz] said both he and Connally are under orders from you to find the easiest money man in town."

On August 4, about two weeks later, Connally reported to Nixon that Burns feared that Treasury was moving to take over the Fed. Connally said he told Burns it was not his goal. Nixon's leaked messages had apparently been received. Burns was now clearly aware of threats to Fed independence, despite Connally's denial.

On October 10, 1971, Nixon and Burns spoke in the Oval Office. Nixon continued to press for flooding the banks even more and raised the concern with Burns that weak economic conditions would hurt his reelection chances.

Nixon: "I don't want to go out of town fast . . . this will be the last Conservative administration in Washington."

Nixon claimed that the "liquidity problem," by which he meant the problem resulting if too much money flooded the banks, was "just bullshit." Burns stated that his monetary policy had produced "lots of liquidity" in the banking sector, again indicating he thought he'd flooded the banks enough.

Burns: "I don't want to see interest rates exploding on the next . . . [garbled]. I could lose control of my Board."

Nixon: "Does this mean we're stuck then with a recession next year?"

Burns: "No, I predict recovery."

Burns was concerned that interest rates might go up dramatically in response to inflation. If inflation worsened, other members of Federal Reserve Board would likely demand a slowdown in the money printing press. With a little more than one year to go before the election, Burns still thought his monetary policy was just right.

Burns Surrenders, November 1971

On November 10, 1971, Burns' abruptly changed his tone after twenty-one months of staunchly resisting Nixon's pressures to flood the banks even more. Burns spoke to Nixon in a private telephone conversation and inexplicably announced a reversal:

Burns: "Look, I wanted you to know that we are reducing the discount rate today."

Burns's board reduced the recommended Fed lending rate to banks, the discount rate, one-quarter of a point to 4.75 percent. Lowering the rate would make money cheaper and more available for banks—flooding the banks with more money.

Burns reinforced his change of opinion on the appropriate Fed policy by announcing he was taking even more aggressive steps to get the Fed's open-market committee to pump even more money into the system.

Nixon: "Great. Great . . . You can lead 'em. You can lead 'em. You always have now. Just kick 'em in the rump a little."

Burns is now completely converted to Nixon's way of thinking.

Burns: "Time is getting short. We want to get this economy going."

One year before the election, Burns was totally on board the Nixon reelection campaign. Time, Burns noted, is critical. It's not merely enough that the economy needed to get going, it needed to get going before the election.

Later in December, Shultz discussed with Nixon a recent conversation that he had had with Arthur Burns. Burns, Shultz tells the President, is upset about the recent nominee to the Federal Reserve Board. Burns's favorite nominee was passed over in favor of the No. 3 candidate.

Nixon: "Now what about the money supply?"

Shultz: "He [Burns] agrees that the money supply should now go up."

Nixon: "Is he going to do it?"

Shortly after, Burns entered the room. After exchanging pleasantries, Burns eventually said, "I've got Federal Reserve problems" and discussed his disappointment in the new nominee. He explained his concern that Connally's views had influenced the decision. Nixon described the decision process, which involved various political considerations, but never mentioned the "easiest money man" criterion. After the men finished the discussion about the appointment process, the meeting seemed to be wrapping up, then:

Nixon: "[garbled] . . . I'm not going to raise this point, but these people have asked me about the money supply. Burns can take care of it. Correct? [garbled]"

Burns: "Burns is on the line."

Nixon: "Arthur, [garbled]. You're independent! [Burns laughs]. Independent! You get it up. I don't want any more nasty letters from people about it. OK?"

Burns: "That [no more nasty letters], I can't guarantee."

Later,

Nixon: "The whole point is, get it [the money supply] up. You know, fair enough? Kick it!"

Three months prior to this conversation, Milton Friedman had warned Nixon about wage and price controls and the temptation they would provide for engaging in expansionary fiscal and monetary policies under the illusion of price stability. Burns was now "on the line" and playing ball. Burns and Nixon were doing precisely what Friedman had warned against. Burns's and the Fed's independence was now a source for jokes.

In February 1972, with less than nine months until the November 1972 election, Nixon, Ehrlichman, and Shultz held a meeting. Burns was not present.

Shultz reported that the "money supply is beginning to move," adding:

> **Shultz:** "The economy *has* to be good, strong expanding economy this year. So much at stake on that. . . . He [Burns] recognizes that [the need for a strong, expanding economy] and he needs to do everything that he can do. . . . Why worry about interest rates going down? . . . We want low interest rates. What's the problem there? So, we don't have a return flow of money from Europe? So what? Keep the money supply going up!"

Nixon and Shultz feared that Burns was insufficiently enthusiastic about keeping the money printing press going, despite his earlier explicit promise. Indeed, Nixon seemed paranoid concerning Burns's loyalty. The numbers for the money supply indicated that the Fed had already become decidedly more expansionary, just as Burns had promised, and that Shultz's and Nixon's suspicions about Burns were unwarranted. Interest rates were dropping. The money printing presses were humming. Over the two months before this conversation, various measures of money were growing at annualized rates in excess of 10 percent, rates certain to intensify inflation down the road.

Why Did Burns Reverse Policy?

In February 1971, Burns told the president, "If we flooded the banks even more than we have, I think you could have awful problems in 1972 and beyond." He maintained his opposition to flooding the banks "even more" until November 1971, when he made a stunning reversal. What prompted this change?

The tapes reveal numerous ways in which Nixon pressured Burns into reversing the policy position that he adamantly defended for years. Nixon appealed to

Burns's loyalty, raised fears that he would be the last "conservative" to hold the presidency, threatened the Fed's independence, and weakened Burns's position in the Fed by appointing people to the Board of Governors who agreed with Nixon's views. In the end, Nixon joked about the Fed's independence to Burns's face and got Burns to "flood the banks more than we already have," against Burns's better judgment. Nixon made it clear that he was the boss in making appointments to the board and put Burns on notice that his power in the administration was falling fast. Apparently, to protect the Fed from Nixon's threats to Fed independence, Burns caved in to all the pressures and gave the president the monetary policy he wanted. The Fed's independence may have been preserved, but the problems that Burns had foretold from flooding the banks "even more" were about to reveal themselves.

The Aftermath

The eventual elimination of wage and price controls in 1973 and the excessively aggressive monetary policy of 1971 and 1972 produced an inflationary boom. The inflation rate measured by the change in the Consumer Price Index for 1973 was 9.6 percent. In response to the post-election Federal Reserve slowdown in the money printing press, the economy swung into a recession in November 1973, one year after the election. The political business cycle boom and then bust had occurred. The recession lasted until March 1975, but even this recession was insufficient to counter inflation. The inflation rate for 1975 was 6.7 percent — higher than the rate that precipitated the earlier wage and price controls. Not until Paul Volcker became chairman of the Federal Reserve in 1979 and initiated the policies that led to the recessions from 1980 to 1982 was inflation finally brought under control. Inflation was finally defeated, but at huge economic cost.

Once inflation gets going it becomes extremely difficult for a sitting president to accept a slowdown in the money printing press that will create a recession. Jimmy Carter said the following in a 1978 televised address about fighting inflation:

There are two simplistic and familiar answers which are sometimes proposed—simple, familiar, and too extreme. One of these answers is to impose a complicated scheme of Federal government wage and price controls on our entire free economic system. The other is a deliberate recession which would throw millions of people out of work. Both of these extreme proposals would not work, and they must be rejected.[4]

Ironically, the latter "unworkable" solution was implemented by Carter's second appointee to chair the Fed, Paul Volcker, and it brought inflation under control. The lesson is simple: avoid getting inflation going. The best way to do this is to keep the Fed independent and the power to control the money printing press out of the reach of politicians.

Summing Up

The Nixon-Burns political business cycle put the nation on an inflationary course that required three recessions to correct. This whip-lashing of the economy was the primary source of the net costs to the economy.[5] How costly was this? To answer this, we need to make some assumptions. Figure 7.3 shows the unemployment rate over the period 1970 to 1985. How much of the unemployment during this period was the direct result of policies required to fight inflation? Let's assume that when the unemployment rate rose above 7 percent, it was the consequence of slowing down the economy to fight inflation. The bulk of this cost occurred in the 1980 to 1984 period after Volcker hit the stop button on the money printing press, but some abnormally high unemployment also resulted in 1974 and 1975, following the post-election monetary tightening. On the plus side, the Nixon-Burns flooding of the banks boosted employment for perhaps two years (see Figure 7.3). Following the expansionary monetary policy in 1970 and 1971, the unemployment rate dropped below 6 percent. Let's assume the drop in the unemployment rate below 6 percent is the benefit of the Nixon-Burns policy.

---

4. October 24, 1978. http://www.pbs.org/wgbh/americanexperience/features/primary-resources/carter-anti-inflation/.

5. Economists have spent considerable time identifying the costs of inflation. Many of these are redistributive. With unexpected inflation, for example, lenders lose while borrowers gain. I estimate the cost only for the business cycle effect.

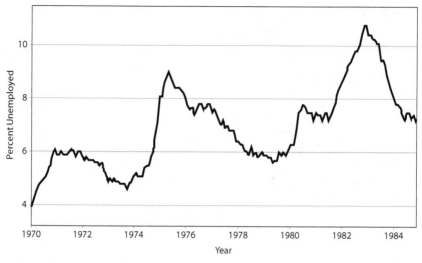

Source: Bureau of Labor Statistics.

Figure 7.3. U.S. Unemployment rate, 1970–1984.

Adding up the time that the unemployment rate exceeded 7 percent and converting this into lost output via Okun's law[6] gives an estimate for lost output and income of around 4 percent of GDP for five years. The Nixon-Burns flooding of the banks lowered the unemployment rate on average about the equivalent of 1 percent for two years. To put this into a more contemporary perspective, if the U.S. economy today lost 4 percent of GDP for five years, the dollar amount would be close to $2.7 *trillion* dollars of lost production and income. The 1 percent reduction in the unemployment rate for two years translates into a 2 percent increase in output and income for two years. In current GDP terms, this would be about $0.5 trillion in increased output and income. The net lost production and income would be over $2 trillion. Even if this estimate is 100 percent exaggerated due to erroneous assumptions, a net cost of one trillion dollars still makes the Nixon-Burns political business cycle one of the top economic blunders of the past hundred years.

Next up, government mismanagement of our environment.

---

6. Okun's Law says that for every 1 percent increase in the unemployment rate (say, from 6% to 7%), national output falls about 2 percent.

8

Environmental Mismanagement
How to Make a River Burn and Other Magic Tricks

"Political pandering comes in all shapes and sizes, but every
four years the presidential primary brings us in contact
with its purest form—praising ethanol subsidies amid the
corn fields of Iowa."
—*Senator John E. Sununu*

ONE OF THE most perplexing and persisting economic problems
facing society is the problem of pollution. Let's look at just three pollution-
related disasters that created a turning point in public concern about the environment: Love Canal, DDT, and the burning Cuyahoga River. Love Canal is a
neighborhood in Niagara Falls, New York, where Hooker Chemical Company
decided to bury 21,000 tons of toxic chemicals, a low-cost solution for its waste
disposal from the company's initial viewpoint. The health and financial costs
imposed on people living in and around this community proved otherwise.
DDT, a suspected carcinogen now banned worldwide in agriculture, was a
widely used insecticide that killed many birds and beneficial insects and greatly
reduced the bald eagle population.[1] In 1969, Cleveland's Cuyahoga River caught
fire as a result of waste dumped by its waterfront industries.

Today, nearly everyone has heard about global climate change and acid
rain. More recently, the hot environmental topic is *fracking*, the fracturing of
subterranean rock formations to facilitate the extraction of oil and gas. Fracking
is now raising environmental and health concerns and may even be responsible
for precipitating an earthquake in Ohio! According to most economists, these

---

1. It is extremely effective in controlling mosquito populations, however, and is still used
in some countries for controlling malaria.

problems have resulted from inadequate governmental regulations. Governmental failure in this area is and will continue to be an economic wreck worthy of a chapter in a book detailing the worst economic policies. The magnitude of damage caused by the blundering is difficult to measure, but it is potentially enormous. In this chapter, two current blunders are reviewed in some detail, one local, the other national in scope. They represent just the tip of the environmental iceberg.

Market and Government Failures

Market failures occur when something goes wrong with market pricing, and incentives lead people to do the "wrong" thing. Pollution is typically given as one possible cause of market failure. When producers and consumers neglect the damage done by their pollution, an economic inefficiency occurs. An item may be produced, for example, that is sold for and worth $10 to the consumer but actually may cost $11 to make if you consider the pollution it creates. The failure to take pollution costs into consideration leads to economic waste, the production of goods that are worth less than their cost. To provide a more concrete example, imagine your dismay in paying cash for a new fully loaded Cadillac, parking it in your garage, and awakening the next morning to find it has been magically transformed into a base-model Chevrolet. You paid, say $40,000 for the Caddy and wind up with a $20,000 Chevy. Pollution-related market failures achieve the equivalent of this uneconomic transformation, taking higher valued goods (in terms of their uses of valuable resources including clean air) and converting them into a lower valued output. Pollution provides a justification for government regulation to set things right.

While decreasing pollution yields benefits, achieving those benefits usually entails costs. If the benefits of reducing a ton of air pollution is $10, economists would frown on taking that action if it cost $20 to do so. This is the equivalent of transforming the Caddy into a Chevy. When you hear economists say that the optimal amount of pollution is not zero, they mean that at some point, before the total elimination of pollution, the cost of reducing it further is greater than the benefit. To put it on a grand scale, does it make sense for a country to spend $100 billion each year to reduce greenhouse gases if other countries go on their merry way, and global climate change is just as big and occurs just as quickly?

Calculating costs and benefits of such things as pollution and their impact on human life is difficult, but it is important if we want to get the prices "right."

Economists usually took for granted, once a market failure was identified, that government would take the appropriate corrective actions. If the production of a good generates \$1 in pollution costs, the textbook solution is for the government to levy a \$1 tax on the producer so that all the costs of production are taken into account.[2] But, when economists investigated regulatory behavior, they discovered that government regulations all too often failed to correct market failures and, still worse, created market failures of their own. Economists have spent a great deal of effort in identifying and in understanding these new failures, *government failures*. Many government failures are highlighted throughout the chapters in this book.

A Case Study: The Mesaba Project

Minnesota, the "Land of Sky Blue Waters," is well known for its vast forests and numerous lakes. Its Boundary Water Canoe Area (BWCA) consists of more than one million acres of limited-access wilderness, where motors are banned in most areas in favor of solitude, canoeing, camping, and fishing. Itasca County, about 80 miles southwest of the BWCA, has 1,000 of Minnesota's 10,000 lakes. Given the county's environmental assets, it is strange that its citizens have been embroiled in an eight-year fight over a proposed massive "clean coal" power plant. The story highlights how and why government mismanages environmental issues and creates government failures and economic wrecks. The project gets the prices wrong and guarantees an unfair outcome.

Acid rain (and acid snow) in the United States is primarily the product of sulfur dioxide (SO_2) from coal-fired power plants mixing with falling rain. Acid rain can severely harm freshwater fisheries, killing off some of the tastiest recreational fish and leaving the acid-tolerant black bass, admittedly a feisty fighter at the end of the line, but lacking something in the fry pan. Acid rain also degrades forests, harms car finishes, poses health risks, and reduces air clarity. Many lakes in the eastern section of the United States have been adversely

---

2. Technically, you want to put the tax on the producer's pollution. If the tax is on the pollution, the producer has an incentive to find a way to reduce the pollution.

affected by acid rain, and regulations to reduce SO_2 emissions have succeeded in reducing lake acidity. Minnesota finally passed a moratorium on acquiring new sources of energy using coal in 2007, but an exemption was made for a "clean coal" power plant in Itasca County, called the Mesaba project.

Scrubber technology has made coal-fired power plants cleaner, but they are definitely not clean. They still produce SO_2 and other health-reducing particulates, as well as mercury. Mercury easily enters the food chain, raising health concerns and producing advisories about the risk of eating fish from waters containing mercury. As acid rain flows through soils in a watershed, aluminum is released from soils into the lakes and streams. Aluminum reduces fish growth. Economic studies also show that residential home prices are adversely affected by proximity to power plants.

So there are many potential negative effects of building a coal-burning power plant. Nonetheless, if benefits from building the plant exceed the costs, economists would support the construction on efficiency grounds. The details of how the costs and benefits actually are assessed reveal major shortcomings in the process, however.

Groups in Favor of the Mesaba Project

Excelsior Energy, the company that is developing the power plant, leads the forces supporting its construction. The only two shareholders (husband and wife) promise that the $2 billion construction project would employ thousands of workers for several years. Many local contractors and building suppliers have lined up in support of the project, as has the local Chamber of Commerce. Over the past eight years, the company has been busy paying salaries to its two owners, reportedly about $300,000 each annually, and conducting activities (including lobbying) to win final approval for the power plant. Most of these funds come from public sources, including a $22 million grant from the Department of Energy, a $9.5 million loan from a local public development fund, and a $10 million grant from the Renewable Development Fund. The two owners of Excelsior Energy contributed a paltry $60,000 of their own capital. Excelsior Energy, it should be noted, has never in its brief history built a power plant.

Excelsior has transferred large amounts of its government grants and loans into the pockets of politicians. State Representative Tom Anzelc summed it up:

These developers have been really successful in capturing public money and getting language and statutory changes giving their company preferential and special treatment. I believe that their highly effective lobbying efforts are directly attributable to the public resources they've had at their disposal. I think they used public dollars to lobby public law-making bodies.[3]

Another opponent of the power plant also summed it up bluntly:

It's a scenario we've seen before: A private company forms to promote a dubious enterprise, hires politically connected lobbyists, sucks up millions in government grants, hands out boatloads of campaign cash to politicians who keep the government money flowing to enrich a handful of lobbyists and consultants—and then the cycle repeats itself over and over.[4]

With their public funds, Excelsior hired a consulting center from the University of Minnesota's Duluth campus to assess the economic impact of the Mesaba Project. Not unexpectedly, the report provided a glowing list of economic benefits, although cautioning that the study was not a full-blown cost-benefit analysis. The key benefit, the study claimed, was the spreading of $200 million to $300 million annually in "value added" across the county. To a county suffering one of the highest unemployment rates in the state, these were welcome words indeed.

Groups Opposing the Project

The forces opposed to the construction of the plant are led by the Citizens Against the Mesaba Project (CAMP), an amalgam of concerned citizens, lakeshore owners, environmentalists, and medical personnel. CAMP members are concerned about health and environmental issues, public financing and

3. Peter Passi, "DNT Investigation: Excelsior Lobbying Cash Questions," *Duluth News Tribune*, September 12, 2011. Retrieved from http://www.camp-site.info/uploads/dnt-investigation.pdf.

4. Karl Bremer, "Campaign cash and army of lobbyists keep 'clean coal' boondoggle afloat for a decade," *Ripple in Stillwater*, August 30, 2011. Retrieved from http://www.camp-site.info/uploads/bremer.pdf.

infrastructure costs, recreational impairment, and the use of eminent domain power that they think was granted inappropriately to Excelsior Energy. The Environmental Protection Agency's environmental impact study for this "clean coal" plant estimates annual pollution output to include 1,200 tons of particulate matter, 1,390 tons of SO_2 and 54 pounds of mercury. Most of the mercury is predicted to fall inside the county.

CAMP receives no taxpayer dollars to wage its campaign against the Mesaba Project. As is so often the case with large groups, it finds it difficult to mobilize individuals into group action. Large groups suffer from what economists call the *free-rider problem*. Individuals realize that adding their own single contribution to the group's activities is unlikely to have any effect on the outcome, while participation in the group's activities is personally costly, involving time and money. So many people are apathetic and abstain from taking an active role in group action. This is especially true with the Mesaba Project, which promises to bring so many dollars and jobs to a county that is hurting economically.

Complicating the political picture is that many owners of lakeshore properties have primary residences outside the county and consequently have no vote in local elections. These nonresident property owners have much to lose from environmental degradation but suffer from "taxation without representation."

Volunteers for CAMP undertook a critique of Excelsior's economic impact study, finding gross misrepresentations of information. Economic benefits to the county, it turns out, were exaggerated by twenty- to thirty-fold. On completion of the plant, only 107 full-time jobs would remain. The most glaring misinformation in Excelsior's study was the claim that $200 million to $300 million in economic value added would be spread annually across the county. Almost all of this "value added" money is interest on the $2 billion project— monies that would go to bond holders and provide no benefit whatsoever to the county. Another major value added item is the purchase of coal (imported from other states). These items are indeed "value added" by an accounting rule, but to say that they are potential economic benefits for Itasca County is, to be excessively generous, misleading. The Excelsior study failed to mention the one major item that would be spread annually across the county: pollution. When CAMP presented its critique of Excelsior's economic impact study at a hearing in the state capital, the economist who donated his services and discovered the accounting misrepresentation was branded "an East Coast elitist" by one state representative. Records show that this representative just happens to be one of the many beneficiaries of Excelsior's campaign contributions.

Federal Government to the Rescue?

The federal government weighed in on the Mesaba Project, too, concerned that the power plant just a hundred miles from the BWCA's recreational wilderness area might adversely affect air clarity. Excelsior quickly resolved this problem. Plans were redrawn to lower the height of the smokestack to reduce particulate matter that might reach the recreational area. This, of course, worsens the environmental impact for Itasca County and surrounding landowners. The power company put an ingenious spin on the decision by announcing that they lowered the stack height for "aesthetic" reasons. The company surely did not want to impose a visual blight on the community.

State Government Ineptitude

At the state's Public Utility Commission (PUC) hearing in St. Paul, members focused on the cost of power generation at the proposed plant and whether or not to force a power purchasing agreement (PPA) on utilities for their output. PUC members were political appointees. It wasn't clear if any of them had taken an economics course, but it was clear they were omitting any consideration of pollution costs in their deliberations. Failure to include environmental costs helps to ensure an inefficient and unfair regulatory decision.

Mesaba Project Postscript

The decision on the Mesaba Project depended heavily on whether or not a PPA could be forced on utilities. The PPA would require power distributors to purchase the Mesaba Project's output and pass costs on to consumers. Minnesota Power, the largest power distributor in northeastern Minnesota, took the lead in objecting to a PPA, calling Mesaba's output unnecessary and too expensive. In October 2012, Minnesota Power's position was revealed to be self-serving when it unveiled a plan to construct a massive power line to bring electricity to northeastern Minnesota from Manitoba.

At the end of 2012, the Mesaba Project was still under consideration, although its owners morphed it into a natural gas power plant. Given Minnesota Power's newly revealed plan to bring Manitoba electricity into the region, clearly one of these projects, if not both, is unnecessary. But all taxpayers should wonder why millions of dollars in cash and regulatory subsidies were given to the Mesaba Project. Failing to incorporate environmental and neighborhood costs of power generation from the coal-based Mesaba Project grossly underestimated the costs and pricing of its electricity. If built, the coal-based Mesaba project would have been in the business of converting Caddies into Chevys. But Mesaba is small potatoes compared to other environmental blunders.

The United States and Oil Consumption

The United States is one of the world's largest oil producers, extracting some 7.8 million barrels of oil every day. While it accounts for only 4.5 percent of the world's population, the United States produces more than 10 percent of the world's oil. Only the Arab League, Russia, and Saudi Arabia produce more barrels per day. Although the United States is an oil-rich country, its oil appetite far exceeds its production. U.S. consumption is 18.8 million barrels per day, so more than 10 million barrels of oil a day must be imported to meet U.S. demand.

When the U.S. consumption of oil is compared to other countries with similar incomes and climates, Americans appear to be oil gluttons. Germany, the United Kingdom, and Switzerland, in comparison, consume about 32 barrels per day per 1,000 people whereas the United States consumes 69 barrels per day per 1,000 people. Only 4.5 percent of the world's population, Americans consume nearly 26 percent of the world's oil production.

The U.S. appetite for oil raises two primary public-policy concerns. First, the burning of gasoline and oil are primary sources of pollutants that cause health problems and greenhouse gases (primarily CO_2), which many scientists have linked to climate change. If all the costs of consuming oil are not taken into account, then a market failure occurs. Second, U.S. dependence on foreign sources of oil raises concerns about supply disruptions and geopolitical conflicts. The Organization of Petroleum-Exporting Countries (OPEC) restricted oil output in the 1970s and shocked the United States into recession. Americans continue to be heavily dependent on foreign oil sources and vulnerable to supply disruptions, however. This helps the government justify maintaining a costly military force in the Middle East to help ensure a smooth flow of oil. Eliminating U.S. dependence on foreign oil would reduce the apparent value of such large expenditures and allow cuts in military expenditures.[5] All told, environmental and geopolitical concerns suggest that a reduction in U.S. oil consumption and dependence has merit. In any event, many members of the major U.S. political parties support reducing oil consumption. If that is the goal, it makes sense to do so in the least costly fashion. Mandates from the federal government requiring automakers to achieve Corporate Average Fuel Economy for their fleets and to foster the use of ethanol in gasoline are two major programs to reduce oil consumption. Both are economically wasteful approaches.

Milton Friedman, Nobel laureate in economics, illustrated a principle for finding least-cost solutions to problems, using a story about an overheated room. One way to reduce the room's temperature is to open the window; another is to turn down the thermostat. Each solution lowers the temperature, but each has a different cost. The moral to the story is that the direct approach, attacking the source of the problem—adjusting the thermostat and reducing the source of the heat—is usually the superior solution. Indirect approaches are usually wasteful.

Few economists would disagree that the most direct approach and the most efficient way to reduce oil consumption is to place a tax on oil.[6] Germany, the United Kingdom, and Switzerland impose stiff taxes on gasoline, a primary derivative of oil. The average citizen is these countries, as noted earlier, consumes less than half the oil of the average American. Of course, few people relish the prospects of paying $7 for a gallon of gasoline, so a major tax on gasoline is vehemently resisted in the United States. The burden of a high gasoline tax could be moderated substantially, however, by lowering income tax rates and providing income tax credits in compensation. The tax would punish gas consumption, and lower income tax rates would reward working. People would have more after-tax income that could be used to continue to consume the same amount of the much higher-priced gasoline if they so chose. The policy, however, would encourage Americans to economize on gasoline usage by buying smaller cars,

---

5. Ivan Eland, *No War for Oil* (The Independent Institute, 2011) reports that adding military costs for "protecting" the gulf might add as much as $5 per gallon to the cost of gasoline.

6. Technically, if the problem is pollution, the tax should be on the pollution not on oil.

living closer to work, and relying more on public transportation. U.S. oil consumption per person would trend downward, and we would become much less dependent on foreign oil. But instead of taking this direct approach to reducing oil consumption, the government has chosen more costly indirect approaches. These indirect approaches are wildly wasteful but politically profitable.

Ethanol: The Upside

One of the most wasteful indirect approaches to weaning Americans off oil is the gasohol program.[7] This program requires that ethanol be added to gasoline in varying proportions. Most gasoline is now E10, containing 10 percent ethanol and 90 percent gasoline; E85 requires a modified automobile engine and contains 85 percent ethanol and only 15 percent gasoline. Ethanol is a pure alcohol, quite suitable as an alcoholic beverage if only a distasteful ingredient wasn't added to prevent it from being imbibed and thus allowing it to escape alcohol taxes. The ethanol program imposes hidden taxes on consumers, has provided billions of dollars in generous subsidies to a grateful special interest group, and makes questionable claims about its environmental benefits while earning points for far-sighted politicians for "solving" our environmental problems. It is a politician's dream, but an economic wreck.

Ethanol can be made from various plant materials, but U.S. ethanol is made from corn. In 2011, about 30 percent of the U.S. corn crop went into ethanol production. Ethanol has a long history as an automotive fuel. The original Ford Model-T ran on ethanol, but automobiles soon switched over to gasoline, a cheaper and higher energy fuel. Figure 8.1 shows that U.S. annual production of ethanol has surged since 1998, increasing from slightly more than one billion gallons to more than 13 billion gallons in 2010. This surge in production and consumption is the result of state and federal mandates requiring its blending with gasoline and the providing of substantial subsidies.

Ethanol has a lot going for it. It is an *oxygenate*, a substance that helps gasoline burn more cleanly, leaving fewer harmful air pollutants. An earlier oxygen additive, MTBE, was shown to have serious negative health effects and was

---

7. Robert Hahn and Caroline Cecot in a 2007 study estimated that the program's costs exceed benefits by billions of dollars annually. See *The Benefits and Costs of Ethanol*, Working Paper 07-17, Nov. 2007, AEI-Brookings Joint Center for Regulatory Studies.

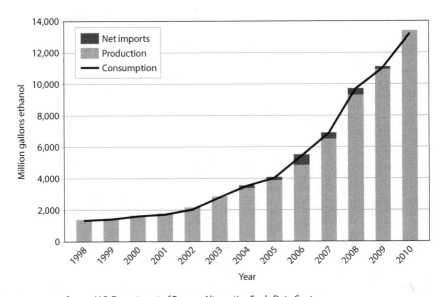

Source: U.S. Department of Energy, Alternative Fuels Data Center.
At www.afdc.energy.gov/afdc/data.

Figure 8.1. U.S. production, consumption and importation of ethanol, 1998–2010.

dropped from gasoline. Enter ethanol. The U.S. Department of Energy states that current corn-based ethanol results in a 19 percent reduction in greenhouse gases and is better for the environment than other gasoline additives such as MTBE. U.S. corn-based ethanol is a U.S. product, reduces our dependence on foreign sources of oil, and is a renewable energy source.

Ethanol: the Downsides

Ethanol has been heavily subsidized by federal and state governments. Not surprisingly, the state governments heavily involved in subsidizing ethanol are corn-growing states. At the end of 2011, the federal government was giving ethanol producers a $0.45 per gallon tax credit plus an additional bonus for small producers. Given that about 14 billion gallons of ethanol were produced in 2011, ethanol producers received more than $6 billion in federal handouts. States add an additional $0.30 or so per gallon in subsidies. Two producers, ADM and Valero Energy, produce about 20 percent of all U.S. ethanol, reaping more than a billion dollars in annual subsidies. They are very generous contributors to political campaigns. In 2011, domestic ethanol producers also received a protective tariff of $0.54 per gallon on imports, but in 2012, the tariff protection expired.

Ethanol production raises food costs. The surge in corn demand from ethanol production has raised corn prices and corn profitability. Land once planted with other grain crops has been shifted into corn production, lowering supplies of other grains and raising their prices. Costs of production—and prices—have also risen for livestock that feed on higher priced grains. These higher prices for food items are a tax on consumers— financial burdens that fall disproportionately on lower income families, which spend a larger proportion of their budget on food items. One nice benefit to politicians is that explicit agricultural crop subsidies have fallen as grain prices have gone up. In essence, the government has shifted the burden of its agricultural subsidy programs off the budget and onto consumers in the form of higher food prices.

The environmental benefits of corn-based ethanol are in dispute. Its proponents rarely consider the environmental costs to manufacture and distribute ethanol. Surging grain output requires the use of more fertilizers, insecticides, and ground water. Agricultural water runoff also imposes environmental costs. Farm machinery uses gasoline and diesel fuels to grow corn. Ethanol is also costly to transport; it is unsuitable for pipelines and must be delivered by ground transportation that uses fossil fuels as well. All told, the environmental costs of corn-based ethanol may be just as high as gasoline itself.

Drivers using gasoline blended with ethanol may find that their cars get fewer miles per gallon.

> That [MPG] decrease can be as high as 10% with E10. If the E15 standard is adopted, mileage will drop even further. The result is that drivers pay the same, or in some cases more, for a gallon of fuel only to find that they have to stop at the gas station more often.[8]

Also, evidence shows that ethanol-blended gasoline damages small engines. Ethanol attracts moisture and contributes to rusting of internal engine parts; it also causes plastic and rubber parts to deteriorate. One manufacturer of a

8. "As Demand For Ethanol Grows, ADM and Valero Will Reap the Benefits" *24/7 Wall St.*, May 4, 2010. Retrieved from http://247wallst.com/2010/05/04/as-demand-for-ethanol -grows-adm-and-valero-will-reap-the-benefits/#ixzz1i2YM0CLT.

weed whacker recently issued a recall of its product because ethanol-blended gasoline produced leaks in gasoline lines that resulted in dangerous spillage. Mercury Outboard Motors offers a caution about using ethanol-blended gasoline in its motors:

> You should be aware of some of the adverse effects that can occur . . . alcohol in the gasoline can absorb moisture from the air, resulting in a separation of the water/alcohol from the gasoline . . . gasolines containing alcohol may cause increased corrosion of metal parts, deterioration of rubber or plastic parts, fuel permeation through rubber fuel lines, starting and operating difficulties . . . it is recommended that only alcohol-free gasoline be used where possible.[9]

To avoid ethanol in gasoline, consumers usually need to purchase higher octane, much higher priced premium gasoline.

Summing Up

Economists acknowledge a potentially useful role for government to correct market failures. Pollution is one area where most economists agree that properly designed regulation could provide net benefits to society. Helping markets to get prices "right" helps to prevent converting Cadillacs into Chevrolets. The stories of the power plant in northern Minnesota and ethanol provide just two examples of government's failure to get it right. There are many more because the institutions we have in place to make environmental decisions do not give rise to a careful weighting of benefits versus costs. Instead, they give rise to a convoluted process that seriously diverges from such a careful weighting and hence we get fleets of Chevrolets when Caddies would be possible.

For the power plant, environmental costs are neglected, and millions of dollars in subsidies are given in the name of developing a "clean coal" power plant. The true cost of producing this electricity, if the plant is built, will be much higher than its price to consumers.

The recent nuclear power plant disaster in Japan and the resumption of nuclear power plant construction in the United States provide yet another example

---

9. *Mercury: Outboard Operation, Maintenance and Warranty Manual*, 2009, 52–53.

of a government-induced market failure in electricity generation. The Price-Anderson Nuclear Industries Indemnity Act (recently extended to all plants built before 2025) provides companies with nuclear power plants a subsidy by limiting their financial liability in the event of a nuclear disaster. Nuclear power plants could not afford full insurance against disaster and, even if such contracts could be written successfully, it is doubtful that a private insurer could honor the contract if a serious meltdown occurred. The federal government had to bail out the insurer AIG after it was unable to honor its insurance contracts for mortgage-backed securities. A major loss from a meltdown undoubtedly would require a similar government bailout. While a meltdown is an extremely low probability event, when one occurs, the economic losses are enormous. Providing subsidies to nuclear power plants contributes to getting the price of nuclear-generated electricity wrong.

For gasoline, the environmental damage costs and benefits to be derived from less consumption of oil and less foreign oil dependence need to be included in the price of oil to get the price right. This would be the equivalent of lowering the thermostat in the overheated room. Instead, we get wasteful federal mandates for indirect solutions such as the blending of ethanol with gasoline and giving billions of dollars in subsidies to producers of high-cost corn-based ethanol while imposing tariffs on lower cost foreign ethanol. These wasteful indirect approaches are the equivalent of opening windows in the overheated room. Ethanol and cellulosic ethanol (made from nonfood plant material) may turn out to be an efficient way to power automobiles, but to properly determine this, we need to get all the prices right. One hopeful sign, but probably just the by-product of excessive government spending and current budget deficits, is that the multibillion-dollar ethanol subsidy and ethanol tariff expired in 2012. But the ethanol-gasoline blending mandate remains in place *forcing* the use of ethanol and preventing us from getting the price right. If oil consumption has costs that are not already built into its price, let's correct the price and let the market determine the best automotive fuel.

The next chapter discusses the government's role in setting up the biggest recession since the Great Depression, the downturn and economic malaise known as the Great Recession.

9

Government Failure
and the Great Recession

Turning the American Dream into a Nightmare

"Well, I guess I don't buy your premise. It's a pretty unlikely possibility. We've never had a decline in house prices on a nationwide basis. So, what I think what is more likely is that house prices will slow, maybe stabilize, might slow consumption spending a bit. I don't think it's gonna drive the economy too far from its full employment path, though."

—*Ben Bernanke*, Chairman of the Federal Reserve System, July 1, 2005, interview on CNBC, responding to a question regarding the possible popping of the real-estate bubble

IT WAS 2005 and the Great Modern American Land Rush was in full swing. Housing prices had been rising substantially for eight straight years and were continuing to rise rapidly, credit was cheap, and lenders were lending. Jessica and Jim, your typical low-income first-time homebuyers, walked into an office of Countrywide Financial, the nation's largest mortgage lender. They had seen a city townhouse not too many miles from Jessica's place of employment, and she and Jim both thought it would provide a substantial lifestyle improvement over living from paycheck to paycheck in a rented apartment. One problem, Jessica and Jim explained somewhat nervously to the loan officer, was the lack of a down payment and not much credit history. "No problem," the loan officer replied. Jessica and Jim were about to sign a subprime mortgage contract to buy their home. The interest rate would be higher than the prime rates touted in the loan office window, but they were told it was necessary to overcome their lack of down payment.

The monthly payments would keep Jessica and Jim financially strapped for a number of years, but how could they lose? Housing prices were rising 10 percent a year, and their $100,000 house should be worth more than $135,000 in just three years. Whenever they decided to sell the house, they would reap a tidy profit, much more than they could save out of their paychecks. Plus, they were told, they would soon be able to tap into the house's equity using an equity line of credit to buy the new car they wanted. Better yet, the interest payments on their mortgage and on any equity line would be deductible from their taxable income. It was the American dream. They signed the papers.

Countrywide Financial sold Jessica and Jim's mortgage to Fannie Mae, a government-sponsored enterprise created to help channel funds into mortgage lending. Between originating the mortgage and selling it to Fannie Mae, Countrywide Financial made a nice profit, and this gave Countrywide the funds to make another mortgage loan. Fannie Mae, in turn, bundled Jessica and Jim's mortgage with several thousand others and sold off "shares" in the bundle to banks and other investors. Fannie Mae guaranteed the principal and interest on the shares and had no trouble finding eager buyers. Fannie Mae too made a tidy profit and was now ready to buy more mortgages from Countrywide Financial and other loan originators. Everything seemed fine while real estate prices were climbing. But then the unthinkable happened: Real estate prices started to sink in 2006, turning the American dream into a nightmare.

Jessica and Jim are fictitious borrowers for this illustration, but their story was real for millions of customers of Countrywide and other mortgage lenders. Millions of households like Jessica and Jim's got in over their heads financially and eventually defaulted and walked away or were evicted from their bad real estate investments. Some of these households had entered into ill-advised variable rate mortgage contracts with initial low interest payments that ballooned over time. Others signed up for interest-only loans that were initially affordable but became unaffordable when principal payments also kicked in. High-income households got into the act as well, buying second and third homes or speculating on rental properties.

Falling real estate prices and rising default rates shocked mortgage markets. Countrywide suffered major losses on the mortgages it held, and its sources of funding dried up. It failed in 2007 and was taken over by Bank of America. Jessica and Jim's mortgage, along with many other defaulted mortgages, were in the bundles that Fannie Mae had "guaranteed." Fannie Mae went under in 2008 and was taken over by the federal government, costing taxpayers more than any other single financial institution failure in U.S. history. The real estate collapse that began in 2006 triggered what is now called the Great Recession.

The Great Recession

The Great Recession, the worst U.S. recession since the Great Depression, officially started in December 2007 according the National Bureau of Economic Research (NBER).[1] The federal government responded with extraordinary monetary and fiscal policies. The Federal Reserve flooded banks with money at an unprecedented rate. In February 2008, a Bush Administration stimulus plan began sending out tax rebates totaling $168 billion. In early 2009, the Obama Administration passed through Congress the American Recovery and Reinvestment Act, which pumped into the economy $787 billion in government spending and tax cuts, the largest peacetime fiscal stimulus in our history.

Despite these record-setting textbook solutions to fighting recessions, the economy barely budged. The NBER made it official that the Great Recession ended in June 2009, but there was no joy in Mudville, as the unemployment rate stayed nearly twice normal and economic growth remained anemic. Traditional monetary and fiscal policy actions simply were ineffective, or the Great Recession was just much more severe than almost anyone had imagined.

Most economists believe that the Great Recession was triggered by a financial crisis, a freezing up of financial markets that led banks and other lenders to curb drastically their willingness to make loans. This, in turn, reduced spending throughout the economy. While the details of this financial crisis will be studied and debated for decades, it is already clear that the real estate bubble and its bursting played a key role. The Financial Crisis Inquiry Commission (FCIC), issued its 409-page report in January 2011, concluding that the financial crisis was caused by failures in financial regulation and supervision, failures of

---

1. The NBER is the agency entrusted with dating business cycles. "A recession is a significant decline in economic activity spread across the economy, lasting more than a few months, normally visible in real GDP, real income, employment, industrial production, and wholesale-retail sales." Source: http://www.nber.org/cycles.html. The recession is over when economic growth resumes, not when full employment is reached.

corporate governance, excessive risk taking in borrowing and lending, a government that was ill prepared for the crisis, a systemic breakdown in accountability and ethics, collapsing mortgage-lending standards, the misuse of derivatives (new types of financial assets), and the failure of credit-rating agencies to correctly assess risk.[2] Thus, the FCIC viewed the financial crisis as a system-wide failure, the product of a multitude of private- and public-sector errors that produced excessive risk taking in loan markets. Interestingly, the FCIC's findings play down the roles of the government-sponsored enterprises (GSE's), Fannie Mae and Freddie Mac, and federal legislation that encouraged risky lending practices. While many factors undoubtedly contributed to the real estate bubble, this chapter focuses on GSEs and government policies that set the stage and nourished the bubble. Without the real estate bubble, the Great Recession would have been avoided. So, linking government policies to the bubble links it to one of the most costly recessions in U.S. history.

Prohibition was a paternalistic/maternalistic policy to engineer a better society by preventing the sale and distribution of alcohol. The Great Real Estate Bubble was nourished by paternalistic/maternalistic policies to engineer a better society by greatly expanding home ownership, especially to the young and lower income groups. In contrast to government's role in Prohibition, government became a "pusher" during the housing bubble. The government's policy drugs hooked millions of lower income Americans on home ownership, indebtedness they could ill afford, and eventually, it led many of them into bankruptcy. The economic damage done to the young and less fortunate added another cruel dimension to the economic catastrophe.

Economic Bubbles

Economic bubbles occur when excessive enthusiasm or irrational exuberance overtakes a market and drives up the price of something beyond good reason. Bubbles can affect any kind of a market. They can hit commodities such as gold and silver, financial assets such as shares in common stocks, or even swamp land in Florida. When an economic bubble pops, the price of the bubbled good usually drops precipitously. Bubbles are easy to identify after the fact, but while

---

2. *The Financial Crisis Inquiry Report (authorized edition)* (New York: Public Affairs, 2011), xvii–xxv.

the bubble is building, most people don't see it, and they get caught up in the enthusiasm. Ben Bernanke, the well-respected economist and head of the Federal Reserve System, apparently was fooled just like most people in missing the housing bubble.[3] Bubbles occur frequently and regularly enough to suggest they are the products of something deeply engrained in the human psyche.

One of the first documented bubbles occurred in Holland in the seventeenth century. Newly introduced tulips became wildly popular, and the prices of the rarer tulip bulbs were bid to astonishing levels. It doesn't seem like a good idea now, but some unfortunate people purchased one rare type of bulb for the equivalent of 1,000 pounds of cheese or about ten times the annual wage of a skilled craftsperson. These individuals were soon to learn a costly lesson.

As the bubble inflates, owners of the bubbled good feel very good, especially if the bubbled good is an important component of their wealth. If the bubble significantly increases wealth, consumption increases, and savings decrease. After all, why continue to save so much from your income while you have a nice nest egg building? When the bubble bursts, the process reverses. Wealth and consumption both decrease. The bursting of the bubble and the resulting decrease in consumption can have disastrous effects for the economy. This brings us to the U.S. housing bubble of 1997 to 2006.

The U.S. Housing Bubble: 1997–2006

The purchase of real estate is the biggest investment most families ever make, and a house is often a family's largest source of private wealth.[4] A family's real-estate wealth is the *net worth* of its real estate ownership, the difference between the market value and the debt still owed on the real estate. Nearly half of U.S. household wealth in 2008 was derived from real estate. Total wealth of U.S. households was $52.9 trillion and, of that, $25.3 trillion was real-estate wealth.[5] To help put this into perspective, in 2008, the household wealth in real

3. One of the golden rules of being a central banker or President is always display confidence. Hence, Ben Bernanke may have seen the popping of the bubble on the horizon, but perhaps didn't want to destabilize markets by his remarks.

4. For many families, public wealth in the form of Social Security and Medicare are their biggest wealth items.

5. Matteo Iacoviello, "Housing Wealth and Consumption," Board of Governors of the Federal Reserve System, International Finance Discussion Papers, Number 1027, August 2011. http://www.federalreserve.gov/pubs/ifdp/2011/1027/ifdp1027.pdf

Real House Price Index

Source: Derived from Case-Shiller home price indices data. (The author thanks James Butkiewicz for his assistance in constructing this figure.)

Figure 9.1. Housing prices adjusted for inflation.

estate was equal to twice our national income from wages, salaries, interest, rent, and profits.

Although housing prices have shown fluctuations over the period 1890 to 1997, the *real* or inflation-adjusted price of a house has, on average, remained remarkably constant. Figure 9.1 shows that the inflation-adjusted price of a house increased a mere 10 percent between 1890 and 1997, and the inflation-adjusted price held steady between 1954 and 1997. Starting in 1997, this traditional relationship between housing prices and other prices changed dramatically. In nine short years, the inflation-adjusted price of the average house doubled.

The rapid rise in the value of houses between 1997 and 2006 caused household wealth to increase substantially, and Americans responded by consuming more. Equity lines of credit and equity loans backed by real-estate wealth gave home owners ready access to spending power. From the start of 1996 to the end of 2006, household debt increased from 73 percent of our total national production (GDP) to 111 percent. Americans went on a spending spree, believing their

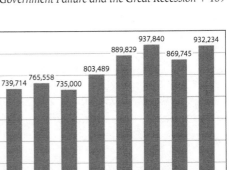

Source: U.S. Foreclosure Market Report.

Figure 9.2. U.S. properties with foreclosure activity.

wealth in real estate was real and permanent. And many lower income people who did not own a home scrambled to buy one, aided by low interest rates, lowered lending standards and the availability of subprime loans. They hoped to share in the American dream before they were priced even further out of the market. Then the bubble burst.

Economists date the peak of housing prices to the late spring of 2006.[6] The drop in house prices was not as dramatic as a bursting bubble but more like a slow leak from a tire. Some thought it was just the beginning of a normal correction after a decade of dramatic home price increases. But the decline in housing prices continued, and foreclosures steadily rose, as increasing numbers of people walked away from their bad investments. Financial institutions that held mortgages suddenly found they were holding toxic assets. Lending standards tightened, which reduced housing demand and put yet more downward pressure on housing prices. Foreclosure activity increased throughout 2007 (Figure 9.2) and would continue to rise in the following years.

6. Robert J. Shiller (2008), "Historic Turning Points in Real Estate," Cowles Foundation Discussion Paper No. 1610.

On October 9, 2007, some eighteen months after the peak in real estate prices, the Dow Jones Industrial Average, usually an advanced sensor of recessions, peaked and began a torturous fall. Now the two primary sources of household wealth, real estate and financial assets, were falling in earnest. Between April 2007 and January 2009, American households lost about $16 trillion or 25 percent of their wealth. The drop in wealth sent consumers into panic mode, lowering consumption spending and reducing spending throughout the economy.

Traditional sources of lending dried up as banks began adding to their cash reserves rather than making increasingly risky loans to individuals and firms. By 2011, after five years of falling housing prices, the inflation-adjusted house price had returned to its historical average.[7] What the bubble had given, the bursting bubble had taken away. While wealth dissolved, household debt had not, and now many homeowners also found their homes under water, worth less than the amount of their mortgage. Cruelly, many if not most of these under water homeowners were lower income families who had been late arrivals to the housing party. In February 2011, 15.7 million homes, 27 percent of mortgaged single-family homes, were under water. In 2012, half of homeowners under age forty who still were in their homes were under water. Table 9.1 provides a brief chronological summary of important events that unfolded during the Great Recession.

Fannie Mae and GSEs

GSEs are federally chartered organizations designed to increase lending to specific groups or sectors of the economy. The Federal National Mortgage Association, commonly called Fannie Mae, is a GSE created by an act of Congress in 1938 to help the ailing real estate market during the dismal economic years following the Great Depression. Fannie was joined by a younger GSE sibling, Freddie (Freddie Mac—the Federal Home Loan Mortgage Association), fathered by the federal government in 1970. Fannie and Freddie's federally mandated mission was to increase the flow of funds going into mortgages by buying mortgages originated by banks in order to allow them to make more

---

7. Figure 9.2 shows that the real value of a home can go even lower than its long-run average for years at a time. So it is possible that the decline in housing prices may continue.

Table 9.1. The Unfolding of the Great Recession

2006	Home prices begin to fall (spring). No federally insured banks fail.
2007	Home foreclosures begin rapid rise; stock market peaks (Oct. 9). Recession officially begins (December); three federally insured banks fail; NBER declares the economy in recession (December).
2008	Stock market (DJI) ends year with loss; housing prices continue to drop; Fannie and Freddie go into "conservatorship" (Sept. 7); Lehman Brothers fails (Sept. 15); AIG bailed out; 30 federally insured banks fail.
2009	Housing prices continue to fall; Stock prices hit bottom in March with prices down nearly 50% from 2007 peak; 148 federally insured banks fail; NBER declares recession over (June).
2010	Housing prices continue falling. 154 federally insured banks fail.
2011	Housing prices stabilize in beginning of year; unemployment remains high and economic growth weak; foreclosures climb.

loans.[8] Most of the discussion that follows focuses on Fannie but applies in most cases to Freddie as well.

Fannie isn't your ordinary bank. Fannie accepts no deposits but rather obtains funds by borrowing, primarily by issuing bonds. Fannie also bundles mortgages, then sells shares in the bundles (a process called *securitization*) to investors and banks. The shares are backed by the mortgages in the bundle, and so are called *mortgage-backed securities*. As a sideline, Fannie acts as an insurance agency, insuring the principal and interest of the mortgaged-backed securities.

In 1968, Fannie was formally separated from the U.S. government to become a private shareholder-owned company. Apparently, the move to privatize Fannie was politically driven. The Johnson administration wanted Fannie off the books so her borrowings would not be counted in the public debt.[9] But even as a private company, her special relationship with the government continued. For example, five members of her board of directors are presidential appointees, something unique for a publicly traded private company. Fannie also receives special regulatory favors. Banks are restricted in the amount of money they

---

8. Savings and Loan Associations wanted a GSE that focused on their mortgages, and this led to Freddie's creation.

9. V.V. Acharya, *Guaranteed to Fail* (Princeton: Princeton University Press, 2011), 17.

can lend to any one borrower, except for GSEs and the U.S. government. In addition, banks that hold Fannie's bonds or mortgage-backed securities are permitted to hold much less capital as a protection against loss from Fannie's debt. So the federal government implicitly declares Fannie's debt to be safe, essentially the equivalent of U.S. public debt and provides regulatory favors to boost the attractiveness of investing in this debt.

Fannie is also permitted to operate with much less capital than traditional banks, and GSE status means exemption from state and local taxation. These subsidies and special regulations, along with a widely accepted belief that the federal government would guarantee Fannie's debt in the unlikely event of a default, created a ready market for Fannie's bonds and mortgage-backed securities. Fannie was able to borrow at interest rates almost as low as the U.S. government and to make tidy profits, at least in the good times. While Fannie's anthropomorphized name may conjure up an image of a beloved family member, few relatives could have achieved what she did: the most costly taxpayer loss for a single financial institution failure in U.S. history.

Although not a traditional bank such as a commercial bank or savings and loan association, Fannie still engages in banking activities. Like a traditional bank, she is a financial intermediary linking savers and borrowers. Like a savings and loan association, Fannie Mae invests heavily in mortgages, but traditional banks or finance companies originate the mortgages and sell them to Fannie. Like a traditional bank, Fannie owes money to others, but to lenders who bought bonds rather than to depositors. Financial intermediaries that are similar to but not traditional banks are called *shadow banks* or *non-bank banks*.

From her inception, Fannie was designed to increase the flow of funds into the residential mortgage market. During the 1930s, banks became reluctant to make residential mortgage loans, and the collapse in residential construction put the brakes on economic recovery. Fannie stood ready to buy eligible mortgages from banks, boosting their confidence and helping to revitalize mortgage lending. Crucial to the process are the standards imposed on borrowers to obtain a mortgage: Did mortgage borrowers make a substantial down payment? Did their income histories give confidence that their borrowings would be repaid? Lending standards provide a natural limit to the total number of borrowers who can qualify for loans. If homebuyers are required to make a 50 percent down payment on a home and have an excellent credit record, few mortgage loans will be made. If buyers are allowed to put nothing down and have a poor or no credit record, the total amount of mortgage loans will be substantially higher—that is, if lenders can be persuaded to make these more risky loans.

During Fannie's first sixty years, real estate prices moved with prices in general. Then in 1997 something changed. The demand for mortgage loans rose, along with the willingness to supply these loans. Much more money was allocated to mortgage loans, and the riskiness of the lending rose, too. The real estate market was off to the races. The following sections detail the laws and regulatory changes that added to the boom in the housing market.

The Community Reinvestment Act (CRA) of 1977

The Community Reinvestment Act (CRA) sought to correct discrimination in the mortgage market by ensuring that all people, regardless of race or neighborhood of residence, would have equal access to bank loans. The act also required that lenders continue to follow safe and sound financial practice. Thus, the criteria for loans were mandated to be the same for everyone, something few citizens would think unreasonable. As carrots and sticks to help enforce compliance, federal scoring of banks was used when deciding merger and acquisition requests: Fail the CRA scoring and kiss any merger plans goodbye; pass CRA scoring and your expansion plans would not be blocked, at least not under CRA.

In 1992, evidence on mortgage lending suggested that CRA guidelines were not being followed. Economists at the Federal Reserve Bank of Boston found that minorities were much more likely to be denied on a mortgage application than white people.[10] Whites had a denial rate of 11 percent whereas minorities had a denial rate of 17 percent, even after taking into account financial, employment, and neighborhood characteristics. The findings suggested that substantially more regulatory enforcement of CRA was needed to level the playing field for bank loans.

Critics of the Boston Fed's study pointed out that the default rates for whites and minorities were running about the same. If racial discrimination prevented

10. Alicia H. Munnell, Lynn E. Browne, James McEneaney, Geoffrey M. B. Tootell, "Mortgage Lending in Boston: Interpreting HMDA Data," Working Paper No. 92-7, Federal Reserve Bank of Boston, October 1992. Retrieved from http://www.bostonfed.org/economic/wp/wp1992/wp92_7.pdf

qualified minorities from getting loans, we might expect default rates for minorities to be lower than for whites. Equal default rates suggested that some important factor may have been overlooked, biasing the Boston Fed's finding. Nonetheless, the federal government set out to encourage greater lending to lower and moderate-income borrowers.

The importance of failing a CRA scoring took a major leap forward with the Riegle-Neal Interstate Banking and Efficiency Act of 1994, which permitted banks to branch across state lines. A bank could now expand from coast to coast, something most easily accomplished through mergers and acquisitions. Economists widely supported interstate branching as it helps to diversify a bank's market and make it less vulnerable to any local adverse economic conditions. But if a bank had aspirations to expand across state lines and to become bigger, the cost of failing a CRA scoring had just gone up, way up.

FHEFSSA of 1992

At about the same time that the Boston Fed's findings were published, the Federal Housing Enterprises Financial Safety and Soundness Act (FHEFSSA) was signed into law by President George H. W. Bush on October 28, 1992. The act established mission goals for Fannie and Freddie. The title of the act mentions "safety and soundness," but the act had contrary intentions. Fannie and Freddie now were expected to make more purchases of risky loans to low- and moderate-income families. "Affordable housing goals" were set, and Fannie and her younger brother Freddie were given guidelines for the percentages of mortgages that they were to purchase from low- and moderate-income families and "underserved" areas. From 1993 through 1995, 30 percent of the mortgages purchased should be from low and moderate income households, and 30 percent also should be from underserved areas (mostly inner-city locations). These percentage goals were to rise yearly. By 2006, the goals were 53 percent of mortgages purchased were to be from low- and moderate-income families, and 38 percent were to be from underserved areas.[11] So throughout the real estate bubble

---

11. Acharya, V. V., M. Richardson, S. Van Nieuwerburgh, and L. J. White. 2011. *Guaranteed to Fail: Fannie Mae, Freddie Mac, and the Debacle of Mortgage Finance.* Princeton University Press.

period, Fannie and Freddie were steadily and increasingly providing an outlet for mortgage originators to make and unload mortgages that were riskier than traditional or prime mortgages.

New types of mortgages were introduced that increased access to loans for lower income people and provided more borrowing power for households that wanted to spend more for a house than a traditional mortgage would permit. These new mortgages required lower down payments or variable rates on interest, starting with an artificially lower initial "teaser" rate that made payments affordable to lower income families. What followed was a surge in loans characterized as subprime. Subprime loans are riskier than prime loans due to lower down payments or higher loan-to-income ratios for borrowers than traditional or conforming mortgages.

Figure 9.3 shows the growth in subprime loans and the total percentage of the mortgage market consisting of subprime loans. Subprime loans started rising

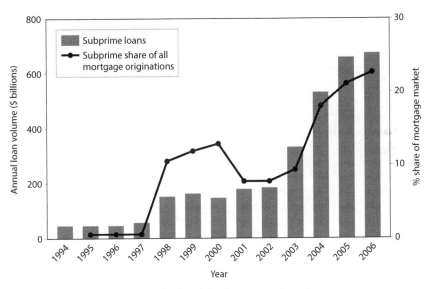

Note: Annual loan volume (left side scale) and percentage share of mortgage market in subprime loans (right side scale).

Source: Inside Mortgage Finance.

Figure 9.3. Subprime Mortgage Market Growth and Share of Total Mortgage Market.

rapidly in 1997, the same year the housing bubble began to inflate. Starting from a minuscule percentage of all mortgages in 1996, subprime mortgages grew to nearly 24 percent of all mortgages in 2006.

Fannie and Freddie's Roles

Expansion-minded banks might have thought that making and holding riskier mortgage loans was just a cost of ensuring a good CRA score. Fannie and her sibling Freddie also pitched in to make subprime loans more acceptable to all originators: They went on a subprime shopping spree. Banks could now unload risky mortgage loans on Fannie and Freddie, while still counting them as "good deeds" to boost their CRA scores.

In the ten years between 1997 and 2007, Fannie and Freddie tripled the amount of mortgages they owned, raising their total to $1.4 trillion.[12] In addition, their purchases of mortgages became increasingly risky. From 2003 to 2007, when Freddie and Fannie were growing rapidly, 60 percent of their new mortgage activity involved high-risk subprime loans.[13] By September 2008, Fannie and Freddie's combined holding of mortgages totaled $1.52 trillion. Of the borrowings that supported their mortgage purchases, $520 billion were short-term borrowings with maturities of less than one year. Like the traditional bank, Fannie and Freddie were vulnerable to a bank run.[14] If the short-term lenders smelled a financial problem, they could "withdraw" their funds as loans matured. This would require Fannie and Freddie to sell off hundreds of billions of dollars in mortgages to accommodate the loan withdrawals—using mortgages whose values were already falling fast in the market due to defaults and rising default risks. Fannie and Freddie were also in deep trouble as a result of impending insurance losses from the guarantees they made on mortgage-backed securities. It was clear that they were bankrupt.

This spelled trouble for traditional banks as well. In the previous ten years, banks had steadily increased the share of their investments in mortgages and owned some 17 percent of Fannie and Freddie's IOUs. A default would seriously

---

12. Acharya, et al., (2010), 81.

13. Acharya, et al. (2010), 59, table 3.4 and author's calculation.

14. Acharya, et al. (2010), 75.

weaken banks and put them at risk of bankruptcy as well. Compounding the problem is that traditional banks were borrowing almost 30 percent of their funds, and these borrowed funds, unlike their deposits, were uninsured. So, smelling financial problems, lenders to traditional banks quite rationally would begin withdrawing their loans to banks, causing a run on the entire banking system, led again not by depositors but by lenders. A full-blown banking crisis was in the making.

On September 7, 2008, slightly more than a year after the peak in housing prices, Fannie and Freddie went into government conservatorship. A federal fund totally $200 billion was allocated to back their debt obligations. Fannie and Freddie had become too big to fail, and the government did what most people assumed it would do all along—guarantee Fannie and Freddie's debts. In the 1980s, 700 savings and loan associations failed costing taxpayers around $150 billion. Fannie and Freddie alone are likely to cost taxpayers more.

The Federal Reserve's Monetary Policy: A Contributing Factor?

The Federal Reserve, the U.S. central bank entrusted with conducting monetary policy, also may have played a role in fostering the great real estate bubble.[15] Critics of the Fed argue that it kept interest rates too low while the bubble was developing. The Fed directly manipulates short-term interest rates, and adjustable rate mortgages (ARMS) are tied directly to short-term rates. ARMS grew in popularity while the bubble grew, and by 2005, they made up one-third of all mortgages issued.[16] Thus, the Fed's policy of holding short-term rates low helped to draw new homebuyers into the real estate market, lured by cheap financing. While the degree of the Fed's role in creating the bubble is still subject to dispute (denied especially by the Fed), the evidence seems to suggest monetary policy

---

15. Lawrence H. White, "Monetary Policy and the Financial Crisis," in *Boom and Bust Banking: The Causes and Cures of the Great Recession* (Oakland, CA: The Independent Institute, 2012).

16. Barbara Hagenbaugh, "More Homebuyers Go with Adjustable Rate Mortgages," *USA Today,* March 30, 2005. Retrieved from http://usatoday30.usatoday.com/money/perfi/housing/2005-03-30-arms-usat_x.htm.

played some role in aiding and abetting the bubble. If so, the Fed was involved in three of the economic blunders described in this book (see the chapters on the Great Depression and Nixon-Burns for the others).

Summing Up

Many factors contributed to the excessive expansion of mortgage lending, and especially subprime mortgage lending, during the housing bubble. This chapter focused on the government's contribution. The Community Reinvestment Act, with its bank-scoring requirements, made increased subprime lending almost a necessity for expansion-minded banks. The FHEFSSA of 1992 established goals for Fannie and Freddie to purchase subprime mortgages from banks and other mortgage lenders. The financial sector eventually provided what the federal government wanted. Then the music stopped.

According to the FCIC's report, government policies should not get all the blame for the real estate bubble, but clearly policies designed to increase subprime lending contributed. Regulators watched Fannie and Freddie triple their ownership of mortgages in ten short years. And regulators allowed Fannie and Freddie to become two of the riskiest holders of subprime mortgages in the financial system while operating under the protection of and subsidies associated with being GSEs.

Government regulations and regulators failed taxpayers. The costs of this failure go beyond the several hundred billions of dollars in direct losses to Fannie and Freddie. Of greater significance is that millions of households are losing their homes—homes that should never have been built or bought—and millions of jobs are being lost during what is likely to be a decade of post-bubble recession. Adding it all up, the government's role in contributing to excessive subprime lending, the housing bubble, and the Great Recession ranks high among its worst public policies in the past hundred years.

Numerous regulatory questions and problems persist. Do we really need Fannie, Freddie, and the GSEs to redirect credit in the economy? Is it the proper role of government to set percentages of lending that should go to lower income people? Should traditional banks, which receive the benefits of deposit insurance to prevent bank runs, be allowed to borrow funds that once again expose them to bank runs and risk creating financial instability and recession in the whole economy? Isn't anyone in government, either legislators or regulators, going to be held accountable for this economic disaster?

In the remainder of the twenty-first century, the United States is likely to perform economically like old Europe, not the old United States. The economic growth rate is likely to be lower and unemployment rates higher than rates during the last half of the twentieth century. The culprit: the federal government's inability to balance its budget. The next chapter details the problems with Washington's sea of red ink.

10

Decades of Deficits

The Real Red Menace

"Wall Street shares slump as S&P downgrades U.S. debt
outlook: Ratings agency cuts long-term outlook from stable to
negative for first time since Pearl Harbor attack 70 years ago."
—*The Guardian*, Tuesday, April 19, 2011, a page 1 headline

"Markets Brace for Downgrade's Toll"
—*The Wall Street Journal*, Monday, August 8, 2011, 1

AFTER WORLD WAR II, Americans were concerned about com-
munism and the Soviet Union, the *red menace*. The economic collapse of the
Soviet Union proved we were unduly concerned. Now we're discovering that
the real red menace is the sea of red ink piled up by the U.S. government through
deficit spending during the first decades of the twenty-first century. Left un-
checked, this growing debt threatens both U.S. and global economic stability.

In 2000, most economists saw no problem in the federal government's budget deficit. In fact, by one common measure, the government was running a
budget surplus. Now the U. S. government is hampered by debt and deficits
that loom as far as the eye can see, or at least as far as the forecasters can forecast. Budget deficits, spending outlays in excess of tax revenues, have piled up,
especially over recent years, to produce a public debt and forecast for growing
debt that has lowered the credit rating of the U.S. government. What caused
this reversal in fortunes? Numerous factors combined to shift the budget into
the red, including two recessions that reduced tax revenues, a massive fiscal
stimulus plan, wars, tax cuts, and gifts to the elderly. The unifying theme is
the politician's reelection golden rule: provide current benefits and postpone
the costs. Deficit spending fits the bill.

Our government's debt now approaches historic levels. Excessive public debt has sunk more than one country. Will it wreck ours? The prognosis is troublesome. The potential long-run damage that excessive public debt imposes on the economy makes the deficit-ridden start of the twenty-first century a worthy chapter for the worst U.S. public policies. But, unlike most of the wrecks in this book, there is still time to right the sinking ship.

Measuring the Public Debt

Measuring the public debt isn't so easily done. Some news reports will claim the debt is more than 100 percent of our national income, while another report will claim it is only 60 percent. The reason for this is that there are different measures of the public debt. The two most widely used measures of the national debt are *public debt outstanding* (*gross debt*) and *publicly held debt* (*net debt*). Gross debt measures the dollar value of all government bonds and similar obligations that the U.S. government has produced. Net debt subtracts from the gross debt all the debt held by the U.S. government or its agencies. Economists don't agree on which measure of the debt is best. Of the various figures and tables in this chapter, constructed by various governmental and international organizations, some use net debt and others gross debt. Researchers studying the effect of public debt on economic growth and many other economists as well think that gross debt is the better measure of the two. Interestingly, President Bill Clinton, in his last three years in office, is widely credited with running a budget surplus that reduced our public debt. This was true only for the net debt, however, not the gross debt.

A third, less commonly mentioned measure of the national debt includes all the government's unfunded obligations, its promises of future payouts for which sources of revenue have yet to be secured. Most of these unfunded obligations come from Social Security and our government health care programs. This chapter focuses on the gross and net measures of the public debt and the more immediate dangers they pose. Our unfunded obligations are longer term problems for taxpayers and are such enormous wrecks-in-the-making that they received separate chapters of their own (see the chapters on Social Security and Medicare.).

Public Debt: Is There an Optimal Amount?

Shakespeare was wrong when he composed his famous line, "Neither a borrower nor a lender be." Economists and common sense tell us that borrowing and lending are vital to any economy, and government borrowing makes sense, too. Clearly, the optimal public debt is not zero. Why impose taxes on one generation for constructing infrastructure that may last fifty years? Why make taxpayers in the 1940s pay the full cost of World War II when its successful outcome provides benefits to numerous generations to follow? Taxing the current generation for outlays that have long-running benefits runs the risk that current taxpayers will not support or adopt the policy, even when its total benefits over time exceed the total costs. Spreading the costs out over time is economically efficient and arguably fairer as well. But debt can be overdone and economically wasteful. To avoid negative effects on the economy, government outlays and tax cuts that are financed with public debt have to be shown to be worth the money. Borrowing to build a bridge to nowhere reduces economic welfare. Economists now have evidence that excessive public debt also slows the economy's growth. Public borrowing, as with government spending in general, can be a good thing, but lately we have too much of a good thing, at least if we want a healthy, prosperous economy.

The Resurgence of Public Debt, 1970–2010

John Maynard Keynes (1883–1946) and especially his followers, the Keynesians, revolutionized thinking about savings, consumption, and public debt. The dominant economic school before Keynes was the classical school, the group of economists who emphasized savings and wealth accumulation as the key to economic growth and development. While practically all economists agree this is valid in the long run, Keynesians focused on the short run. Keynesians pointed out the recessionary effects of a decrease in private-sector spending and emphasized the need for government spending or tax cuts to boost spending when this occurs. Increasing public debt was a natural consequence of pursuing Keynesian antirecessionary policies, and this created a more lenient attitude toward increases in the public debt. Budget deficits and national debt, which classical economists thought anathema to a healthy economy, became a necessity for Keynesians. Short-run oriented politicians warmed immediately to Keynesian economics. Immediacs took the reins of macroeconomic policy.

In 1971, after imposing wage and price controls on the economy and taking the United States off the international gold standard, President Richard Nixon was quoted as saying, "I am now a Keynesian in economics." Not surprisingly, during the eight years of the Nixon-Ford presidencies the federal budget was always in deficit. The ratio of public debt to our national income, which had been declining since World War II, reversed direction in the 1970s, and the upward trend continued over each of the next three decades. Presidents George W. Bush and Barack Obama combined to make the first ten years of this century "the decade of debt."

The Bush administration boosted public debt with tax cuts, a major Medicare expansion, and wars in Iraq and Afghanistan. The Obama administration continued the wars and temporary tax cuts and intensified the debt orgy with the American Recovery and Reinvestment Act.

Deficits and Debt in Perspective

Figure 10.1 provides more detailed information on U.S. gross and net public debt since 1940. The first and larger of the two columns indicates our gross debt and the second column net debt. Values for the debt are presented at ten-year intervals starting in 1940 and ending in 2010. Between 1940 and 2010, our gross debt increased from $43 billion to more than $13.5 trillion. By November 2012, gross debt jumped to $16.2 trillion, or about $142,000 per taxpayer. The real growth in public debt is actually less dramatic than these numbers suggest as the numbers are unadjusted for inflation. A debt of $43 billion in 1940 is actually more like $670 billion in 2010 dollars. Still, it is clear that the public debt has grown substantially between 1940 and 2012, twenty-four-fold in inflation-adjusted terms.

An alternative and perhaps better way to assess the burden of the public debt is to calculate the debt as a percentage of our national income, a measure of our ability to pay for the public debt. As an example, consider two families, each with a $100,000 mortgage debt. One family makes an income of $40,000 per year, and the other $100,000. The lower income family's debt-to-income ratio

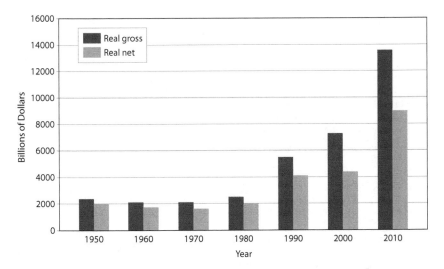

Source: Federal Reserve Bank of St. Louis and author's calculations.

Figure 10.1. Real gross and real net public debt, 1940–2010

is 2.5 while the ratio is 1.0 for the higher income family. While each family has the same debt, the burden is much higher for the low-income family. Figure 10.2 converts the two measures of our public debt into debt-to-income ratio (debt as a percentage of our national income). Prior to our most recent period, our public debt as a percentage of national income, both gross and net, peaked just after the Second World War. At the time, growth in the economy and tax revenues and restraint in deficit spending caused the debt as a percentage of our national income to decline. After 1980, the downward trend reversed. By 2010, our gross debt as a percentage of national income surpassed the debt of 1950. Public debt continues to pile up. In 2012, our gross debt as a percentage of national income exceeded 100 percent.

In 1950, there was no urgent crisis concerning the public debt. Why should we be so concerned about our public debt today? The reason is that our current deficits are expected to persist, taking our public debt still higher. Following World War II, government spending fell dramatically. In contrast, today our government spending is growing rapidly, in part because of attempts to stimulate the economy out of recession but also due to the aging of the population and the promises associated with Social Security and Medicare. The current deficits will not vanish like those following the war without some major cuts

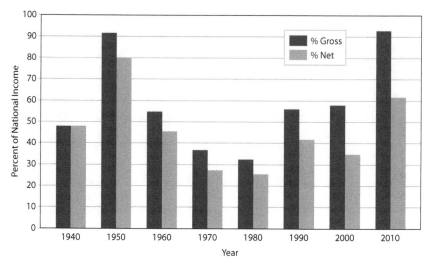

Source: Federal Reserve Bank of St. Louis and author's calculations.

Figure 10.2. Gross and net public debt as a percent of national income (debt-to-income ratio).

in outlays or massive increases in tax rates. Politicians find that cutting benefits or raising taxes now violates the reelection golden rule: give benefits now and worry about costs later. The 2011 negotiation that raised the debt ceiling in exchange for future spending cuts falls far short of making real headway on deficit control. Before the deal, $10 trillion in more debt was projected to accumulate over the next decade. The deal is expected to lower the deficits by $2 trillion to $4 trillion at most. Thus, even with the deal, the debt-to-income ratio can be expected to rise. Regardless, our current debt level is already sufficiently high to adversely affect the economy in the future.

The deficit for the 2011 budget (September 30, 2011 to September 30, 2012) added another $1.3 trillion to our publicly held debt, or about $13,000 more debt per taxpayer. The 2011 deficit represents nearly 9 percent of our nation's production and about 30 percent of total government outlays. Incredibly, for every dollar the government spent in the 2011 budget, it had to borrow 30 cents. The Congressional Budget Office projects that net debt as a percentage of national income will exceed 109 percent by 2023. This is an optimistic guess; the actual amount is likely to be considerably higher. The debt forecast depends heavily on what likely are overly optimistic forecasts for future U.S. economic growth and restraint on entitlement outlays, as well as unrealistically low predictions for future interest rates.

National Debt: International Comparisons

The United States is certainly not alone in the accumulation of public debt. Table 10.1 presents selected international comparisons for net public debt in 2010. Many countries have levels of debt relative to their incomes that are considerably higher than the United States. In fact, adding up all the public debt for all nations and dividing by all the nations' incomes, the average is estimated to be 59.3 percent, a number slightly higher than that for the United States. If the U.S. debt is average, why are we so concerned? The average for the world hides an important fact: Only 35 out of 131 countries had higher public debt relative to their incomes, and many of those countries have experienced or will experience major economic disruptions in the future. The United States is entering dangerous territory for public indebtedness.

Figure 10.3 provides a visual look at the major developed countries and their current gross debts and budget deficits in 2011, both measured as a percentage

Table 10.1. Net Public Debt as percent of national income, 2010 (estimates)

Country	debt (% national income)
Japan	225.8
Zimbabwe	149.0
Greece	144.0
Iceland	123.0
Italy	118.0
Ireland	94.2
U.K.	76.5
World	59.3
U.S.	58.9
Switzerland	38.2
China	17.5

Source: CIA Factbook, 2009.

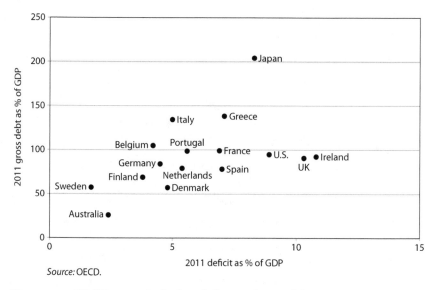

Figure 10.3. OECD countries budget deficits and gross debt, 2011.

of national output (GDP). The vertical axis measures the country's gross public debt as a percentage of national output. Japan leads the way with a gross debt-to-output ratio of 200 percent. That is, Japan's national government's debt is more than twice as large as it national output. The horizontal axis measures the government's 2011 outlays (spending on goods and services and transfer payments like Social Security and Medicare) in excess of its tax revenues. In this measure, Ireland and the United Kingdom are followed closely by the United States as the biggest deficit spenders. The U.S. deficit as a percentage of national output is higher than the deficits for Greece, Portugal, and Spain, three countries suffering severe financial distress. Worse yet, the United States is soon likely to surpass these three countries in gross debt as a percentage of national output; high current deficits push up the total U.S. debt level over time.

Foreign Held Public Debt and the Trade Deficit

As of January 2012, foreigners owned $5.06 trillion of U.S. debt, or 32 percent of the gross debt of $15.6 trillion. The largest holders were China ($1.17 trillion) and Japan ($1.08 trillion). The share held by foreigners has grown dramatically since 1988, when only 13 percent of the debt was held by foreigners.

The foreign ownership of U.S. public debt is symptomatic of a major problem facing the United States: living beyond its means. We see this in our trade deficit. Put simply, the United States imports many more goods and services than it exports. How do we pay for this excess of imports over exports? We pay with financial and physical assets, primarily bonds, stocks, and ownership of steel mills and even highways. Foreigners are rapidly acquiring ownership rights to U.S. assets and the financial obligations of U.S. citizens because we cannot pay for our own level of spending out of our own incomes: We are living beyond our means. The United States is like the old-money family that sells its inherited silver to maintain its membership in the country club. The chief spendthrift in the economy is the U.S. government, spending more than $1 trillion in excess of its tax revenues in fiscal year 2011. Americans and the U.S. government as a group had *negative* net national savings in 2011. We are spending more than our incomes so we borrow from foreigners to fill the gap. If these funds borrowed from foreigners were used to invest in resources that produced the means to repay principal and interest to the foreigners, as was the case in the nineteenth century, the situation would be fine. Unfortunately, most of the borrowings go to raise our consumption. We live relatively better now, but we will pay the foreign piper later. The United States, like the old-money family, is on the decline.

Excessive National Debt: A Drag on Economic Growth

A 2011 poll of the members of the National Association for Business Economics listed the U.S. budget deficit as the No. 1 threat facing the U.S. economy. Recent statistical work by economists helps to justify the concern by finding that large amounts of public debt contribute significantly to lower economic growth. Reinhart and Rogoff, in a 2010 study published by the *American Economic Review,* conclude that "normal" levels of debt seem to have little or no effect on economic growth, but public debt can reach a tipping point after which more debt significantly lowers a country's economic growth. They estimate the tipping point to be a gross debt-to-income ratio of 90 percent.[1] In a recent working paper published by the International Monetary Fund, Kumar and Woo also

---

1. Carmen M. Reinhart and Kenneth S. Rogoff. "Growth in a Time of Debt." *American Economic Review,* 100, no. 2 (2010): 573–78.

find that countries whose debt-to-income ratio exceeds 90 percent have significantly lower economic growth.[2] Caner, Grennes, and Koehler-Geib in a World Bank Conference paper, report results in line with these other studies, but they observe that the tipping point might be even lower. In the first part of 2012, the U.S. gross debt-to-income ratio exceeded 100 percent.[3] If the economic findings concerning public debt and growth apply to the United States, the United States is now beyond the tipping point, and our public debt will be a drag on our future economic growth. Lower economic growth means slower absorption of new laborers into jobs and less success for those unemployed people seeking work. As a result, the normal U.S. unemployment rate can be expected to rise. Slower growth and higher unemployment rates are the legacy of excessive public debt.

Economic theory gives a variety of reasons why larger amounts of public debt would slow economic growth. When the government borrows money, it takes savings from the economy that otherwise would have been channeled to the private sector. Economists say that the government borrowing *crowds out* the private-sector borrowing. Some of the savings siphoned away by the government would have been earmarked for investing in new plants and equipment or new start-up companies. Crowding out the private sector would not be such a problem if the government was borrowing money for public investment projects that raised national productivity. Examples of such spending could include investments in education, research, and infrastructure. The evidence, however, is that much of the borrowing goes into consumption, sometimes rather inefficient consumption, rather than public investment. In any event, evidence is that nations that borrow heavily and move beyond the tipping point are likely to be using the funds in nonproductive ways. As a result of the government's heavy borrowing, those nations face higher interest rates that make growth-enhancing private-sector investments no longer profitable. Statistically, countries with a high level of public debt find that their economic growth suffers.

Another reason government debt might cause a drag on the economy comes from the higher tax rates that are needed to pay the interest on the debt. Higher

---

2. M. Kumar and J. Woo, 2010, "Public Debt and Growth" (IMF Working Papers 1–47). Washington, DC: International Monetary Fund.

3. M. Caner, T. Grennes, and F. Kohler-Geib, 2010, "Finding the Tipping Point: When Sovereign Debt Turns Bad" (Working Paper 5391). Washington, DC: The World Bank Policy Research.

tax rates distort economic decisions and create inefficiencies of their own (see the chapter on Tax Follies). Based on an Office of Management and Budget baseline forecast for 2017, interest payments for the public debt will exceed the cost of Medicare. We see or hear of families that are strapped because of an excessive credit-card burden from financing consumption spending. These families find it impossible to save the funds needed to get out of debt. Governments and nations also can be strained by excessive public debt.

The American Recovery and Reinvestment Act (ARRA) of 2009

Soon after taking office, President Barack Obama signed ARRA into law. It was the single largest discretionary fiscal stimulus plan in U.S history, both in absolute dollar terms and as a share of our national income. ARRA called for $787 billion in spending, transfers, and tax cuts. All $787 billion, representing more than 5 percent of 2009 national income, came from new federal debt creation, much of which was sold to foreigners. Since there are about 140 million taxpayers, ARRA raised each taxpayer's share of the increased federal debt by about $5,600.

The recession that began in 2008 was largely caused by a reduction in Americans' wealth. American consumers were double-slammed by declines in home prices and in the stock market, decreasing wealth by some 25 to 30 percent, or about $25 trillion. Since annual consumption changes about 4 cents for every $1 change in wealth, a reduction in wealth of $25 trillion lowered consumption by about $1 trillion, or 7 percent of national income. This reduction in consumer spending had a spillover effect, reducing the incomes of others, who in turn cut their spending as well. Economists are uncertain about the size of this spillover effect, but it is likely to be at least equal to the initial drop in consumer spending. If so, the total drop in spending would be 14 percent of GDP. Using Okun's law, a statistical rule giving a rough approximation of the relationship between income changes and changes in the unemployment rate, we can estimate that the wealth decrease would raise the unemployment rate 7 percent. This means that, if the unemployment rate was 5 percent before the wealth crash, the unemployment rate would rise to 12 percent, assuming other factors stay the same. But other things did not remain the same. The Federal Reserve, the U.S. central bank, cranked up its printing press, and ARRA kicked in government spending that added $5,600 more public debt for each taxpayer.

The Congressional Budget Office estimates that in 2010, the year in which ARRA had its biggest impact on employment, ARRA raised employment by about 2 million. Let's assume the full effect of ARRA was to raise employment by 3 million for one year. This means each job produced cost Americans $262,000 in more public debt ($787 billion divided by 3 million workers). Worse still, the employment boost attributed to ARRA was only temporary. The end of ARRA caused government outlays and tax reductions to fall to pre-ARRA levels. This produced an equal-and-opposite effect on employment. ARRA bought some employment gains in the short run, but the higher public debt remains for the long run. As we have seen, economic research finds evidence that increases in public debt act as a drag on economic growth. If so, the temporary boost in employment caused by ARRA will be paid for with slower economic growth going forward. We temporarily helped people in the present (current voters, of course) but hurt future generations. It is even possible that losses going forward exceed present benefits. Is it clear that this was a desirable tradeoff?

Summing Up

How costly is excessive U.S. deficit spending in the twenty-first century? The deficit spending may have provided short-run benefits in the form of more jobs and production. This has to be weighed against the long-run costs of slower economic growth caused by the increased public debt. By using the average of other economists' estimates of the effect of public debt on growth, raising the debt ratio from 0.90 to 1.1 might lower growth by 0.35 percentage points. Let's say that U.S. long-run growth is 2.5 percent before the run-up in debt and drops to 2.15 percent after the run-up in debt. If the U.S. economy grows at 2.15 percent, GDP will be 8.4 times its initial value in one hundred years. If the economy grows at 2.5 percent, GDP will increase by 11.8 times its initial value in one hundred years, or about 40 percent more than the slower growing economy. This depends crucially on what happens to our debt-to-income ratio going forward. Reversing the direction for our increasing debt-to-income ratio and bringing us back below the tipping point can stave off the growth-slowing effects. If not, writing in one hundred years, the authors of the sequel to this book, living in the higher debt, slower growing United States would surely classify our debt-producing policies in the first decades of this century a worthy chapter.

This ends the chapters detailing the worst U.S. economic blunders of the past one hundred years. The epilogue wrestles with how the mistakes of the past might provide some guidance for avoiding mistakes in the future.

Epilogue
Can Government Governance Be Improved?

"Little else is requisite to carry a State to the highest degree of opulence from the lowest barbarism but peace, easy taxes and a tolerable administration of justice."
> —Quote attributed to the economist *Adam Smith,* eighteenth century

"We have the best government money can buy."
> —Quote attributed to *Mark Twain,* nineteenth century

IN HIS COMEDIC MOVIE, *History of the World—Part I,* Mel Brooks fires a cinematic shot at critics. The world's first art critic is depicted as a caveman standing high on a rock and urinating down on a wall painted with what would now be considered priceless cave art. It is even easier to be a critic of government policies. To be a creator of art or to be a designer of ways to improve government governance is much more difficult.

Improving government governance is crucial to the lives of billions of people. Bad policies took the United Kingdom from preeminence to mediocrity. Better policies in China lifted more people out of poverty in thirty-five years than a century of European and U.S. foreign aid accomplished in the rest of the world. The United States now finds itself at a crucial stage, and its public policy decisions will determine where the nation stands at the end of this century.

Clearly, some governments govern better than others just as some businesses manage better than others. Factors that promote good government governance, at least as measured by studies of economic outcomes of growth and higher standards of living, include: the rule of law, well-defined property rights, good rules for the central bank, and economic freedom.

The wasteful economic policies identified in this book, policies with costs that exceeded their benefits, were the result of various factors: special interest influences, misguided paternalism, policymaker ignorance, voter ignorance, and the short-run focus of politicians. Can policies be designed to reduce the role of these factors in fostering bad economic policies in the future?

Special Interest Influence

Many of the blunders detailed in this book suggest that special interest money serves as a lubricant for the bad policy machine. Money and campaign contributions seem to have played important roles in explaining the Hawley-Smoot tariff, Medicare Part D, environmental mismanagement, and the poor regulatory oversight of Fannie Mae and Freddie Mac.

Breaking the role of money in politics has been unsuccessful, despite passage of numerous federal laws nominally designed to do so. Every time some campaign finance reform has been passed, loopholes were discovered to circumvent the law. Soft money donations and political action committees now make campaigns more costly than ever. Even when campaign contributions do not come directly into play, retired politicians find lucrative post-public service jobs for themselves or their relatives as lobbyists or influence peddlers.

One of my favorite stories concerns Representative Billy Tauzin (R-LA), chairman of the powerful Energy and Commerce Committee, who played an important role in keeping Medicare's Part D pharmaceutically friendly.

> Though still on a modest Congressional salary [2003], he paid more than $1 million for a 1,500-acre ranch [in south Texas]. And he invited a dozen friends—mostly executives and lobbyists with interests before his committee—to cover its mortgage by paying him dues as members of a new hunting club.[1]

I found this to be a particularly entrepreneurial and entertaining way to monetize political influence.

---

1. David D. Kirpatrick and Duff Wilson, "One Grand Deal Too Many Costs Lobbyist His Job," *New York Times,* February 12, 2010. Retrieved from http://www.nytimes.com/2010/02/13/health/policy/13pharm.html.

Can any public policies be effective in breaking up the "bad policies for sale" business? One way to reduce the role of money in influencing politicians' decisions might be to pay legislators what economists call an "efficiency wage." What if salaries and pensions for legislators were raised substantially on the condition that they would never accept any outside jobs or compensation? This might attract a different breed of politician and diminish the role of special interest groups in buying regulatory and legislative favors. Of course, crafty people will immediately look for ways to circumvent this with lobbying jobs for spouses or children, and other manuevers. So any such law would need frequent review and revision, and still there is no guarantee such a law would succeed.

As long as government grows and continues to broaden its powers in providing legislative profits to special interests (more commonly called *rent seeking* by economists), expect money to matter and campaign spending to continue to set new records. In the final analysis, the best way to break the abuse of money in politics is to have transparency and full disclosures of financial relationships, along with an informed public.

Short-Run Obsession

Short run-oriented politicians produced many of the blunders: pay-as-you go Social Security, Medicare, recklessly large public indebtedness, and the Nixon-Burns political business cycle. Can the negative effects of immediosis be moderated by lengthening and limiting terms of office? Governors of the Federal Reserve Bank serve fourteen-year nonrenewable terms in an attempt to insulate them from presidential and congressional pressures to pursue short-run economic goals that might worsen long-run stability in the economy. Restricting presidents to, say, one eight-year nonrenewable term (with a well-defined recall provision) might help to reduce the preoccupation with short-run policies. U.S. representatives are on a two-year election cycle that keeps them constantly seeking campaign contributions. Lengthening their term and imposing term limits could help.

The Nixon-Burns chapter showed that despite long terms for Fed governors, the Fed still could be manipulated into making politically expedient short-run policy that harmed the longer run interests of the country. It is apparent that more firewalls are needed to keep the Fed independent and on track to serve the best interests of the nation. A rule requiring the Fed to focus only on price stability or a low inflation rate would free it from short-run pressures from presidents and Congress to respond to unemployment. Such a rule would have avoided two blunders: the Great Depression and the Nixon-Burns decade of inflation.

A rule requiring a balanced budget when the economy approaches some reasonable measure of full employment or a rule limiting the national debt to some percentage of national income would restrain government from excessive deficit finance that pushes costs on to future taxpayers.

Paternalism

Governmental paternalism imposes someone's view of the ideal on others in society. Paternalism brought us Prohibition, the War on Drugs, and numerous blue laws. The real-estate bubble was inflated by paternalistic public policies designed to achieve the "ideal" that everyone should own a home. As a result, tens of thousands of lower income persons were encouraged to buy homes that led them into bankruptcy.

President William Howard Taft noted, "No tendency is quite so strong in human nature as the desire to lay down rules of conduct for other people."[2] It isn't obvious how this tendency in human nature can be restrained in the future.

Policymaker and Voter Ignorance

The Great Depression would have been much milder if the Fed's decision makers had better understood monetary economics, especially the severe contraction of the money supply that occurred when depositors withdrew cash from the banks. While our understanding of economics is better, policymaker ignorance could still produce substantial harm. Our burgeoning public debt, which policymakers seem to think is relatively harmless and even essential to getting the economy back on track, may fall into this category.

---

2. Source: http://www.brainyquote.com/quotes/authors/w/william_howard_taft.html.

Policymaker ignorance seems to have also played a role in establishing our pay-as-you go retirement programs. Senator Arthur Vandenberg seemed to honestly believe that establishing a fully funded system was a "leech on society." We now suffer from an unfunded system that has de-capitalized the country and requires major new taxes or repudiation of promised entitlements.

Can policymaker ignorance be corrected? Years of experience with bad trade policies and continued opposition among economists to restraints on trade seem to have had an impact in getting policymakers to produce better policies. Perhaps members of Congress and the president should be required to pass an economics course at an accredited college or university before taking office. Perhaps environmental policies and other spending programs should be put under rigorous independently conducted cost-benefit tests. The findings and methodology could be published and subjected to public scrutiny.

In the final analysis, our public policies will only be as good as our electorate is smart. If our electorate fails to understand policy issues, economics, and history, it is likely to be swayed by plausibly acceptable arguments that yield wasteful policies. The author hopes this book contributes to improving the understanding of the issues so that voters are more informed and better choices are made.

Institutional Arrangements

Does our current sequential presidential primary procedure worsen public policies? I doubt if any candidate in Iowa's presidential primary ever suggested eliminating farm subsidies or the ethanol mandate, at least if she or he had any chance of winning. A policy that benefits one state quite often imposes more costs than benefits on the nation as a whole. As one example, George W. Bush pushed for and achieved steel import tariffs that helped him win Ohio and all its electoral votes. If Bush had lost Ohio in 2004, John Kerry would have been elected president. Ohio also played a role in President Obama's reelection campaign in 2012. He highlighted the fact that he rescued General Motors and Chrysler and saved auto jobs in Ohio. The Electoral College encourages gaming with policies to benefit special interest groups in states that are too close to call, without regard for the best interests of the country as a whole. Abolishing the Electoral College and determining the presidency by popular vote would eliminate this inefficient game playing.

Summing Up

Finding policies to improve corporate governance is not easy. Finding policies to improve government governance may be even harder. Some of the suggestions made here would require constitutional amendments, and there is usually resistance to such change. Many Americans, including politicians, might be happy with the status quo. In such an environment, change is unlikely. But with the insight of hindsight, we can learn from our previous mistakes and attempt to avoid repeating them.

The nineteenth century was Great Britain's century. The twentieth century was the American century. It seems that it is hard to repeat centuries, but it is possible. Or will the twenty-first century belong to the Chinese? The distribution of good long-run economic policies across countries will hold the answer.

References

Abrams, Burton A. "How Richard Nixon Pressured Arthur Burns: Evidence from the Nixon Tapes." *Journal of Economic Perspectives,* 20, no. 4 (Fall 2006): 177–88.

Abrams, Burton A., and James L. Butkiewicz. "The Political Business Cycle: New Evidence from the Nixon Tapes." *Journal of Money, Credit, and Banking,* 44, nos. 2–3 (March 2012): 385–99.

Abrams, Burton, and Siyan Wang. 2006. "The Effect of Government Size on the Steady-State Unemployment Rate: An Error Correction Model" (Working Paper No. 2006-05). Newark: University of Delaware, Department of Economics.

Acharya, V. V., M. Richardson, S. Van Nieuwerburgh, and L. J. White. 2011. *Guaranteed to Fail: Fannie Mae, Freddie Mac, and the Debacle of Mortgage Finance.* Princeton, NJ: Princeton University Press.

Afonso, Antonio, and Davide Furceri. "Government Size, Composition, Volatility and Economic Growth." *European Journal of Political Economy,* 26, no. 4 (2010): 517–32.

Allen, Frederick Allen. 1931. *Only Yesterday: An Informal History of the 1920's.* New York: Harper and Row.

Allen, Frederick Lewis. 1940. *Since Yesterday: The Nineteen-Thirties in America, September 3, 1929–September 3, 1939.* New York: Harper.

Ausick, Paul. "As Demand for Ethanol Grows, ADM and Valero Will Reap the Benefits." *24/7 Wall St.,* May 4, 2010, http://247wallst.com/2010/05/04/as-demand-for-ethanol-grows-adm-and-valero-will-reap-the-benefits/#ixzz1i2YMoCLT.

Ball, Robert M. "Perspectives on Medicare." *Health Affairs,* 14, no. 4 (1995).

Barrilleaux, C. 1997. "A Test of the Independent Influences of Electoral Competition and Party Strength in a Model of State Policy-Making." *American Journal of Political Science* (1997): 1462–66.

Bergh, Andreas, and Martin Karlsson. "Government Size and Growth: Accounting for Economic Freedom and Globalization." *Public Choice,* 142, nos. 1–2 (2010): 195–213.

Boyun, D., and M. Kleiman. 2002. "Substance Abuse Policy from a Crime Control Perspective. In *Crime: Public Policies for Crime Control*, 331–82. Oakland, CA: Institute for Contemporary Studies.

Bremer, Karl. "Campaign Cash and Army of Lobbyists Keep 'Clean Coal' Boondoggle Afloat for a Decade." *Ripple in Stillwater,* August 30, 2011, http://www.camp-site.info/uploads/bremer.pdf.

Burman, Leonard, and Marvin Phaup. 2012. "Tax Expenditures, the Size and Efficiency of Government, and Implications for Budget Reform. In *Tax Policy and the Economy,* edited by Jeffrey Brown, Vol. 26, 93–124. Chicago: University of Chicago Press.

Caner, M., T. Grennes, and F. Kohler-Geib. 2010. "Finding the Tipping Point: When Sovereign Debt Turns Bad" (Working Paper 5391). Washington, DC: The World Bank Policy Research.

Christopoulos, Dimitris K., John Loizides, and Efthymios G. Tsionas. "The Abrams Curve of Government Size and Unemployment: Evidence from Panel Data." *Applied Economics* 37 (10) (2005): 1193–99.

CNNPolitics. "Bush Signs Landmark Medicare Bill into Law." *CNN,* December 8, 2003. http://articles.cnn.com/2003-12-08/politics/elec04.medicare_1_prescription -drug-private-insurers-medicare?_s=pm:allpolitics.

Eland, Ivan. 2011. *No War for Oil.* Oakland, CA: The Independent Institute.

Feldmann, Horst. "Government Size and Unemployment in Developing Countries." *Applied Economics Letters,* 17, no. 1–3 (January 2010): 289–92.

Feldstein, M. "Tax Avoidance and the Deadweight Loss of the Income Tax." *Review of Economics and Statistics* 81, no. 4 (1999): 674–80.

The Financial Crisis Inquiry Commission. 2011. *The financial crisis inquiry report.* New York: Public Affairs.

Fisher, Irving. 1926. *Prohibition at Its Worst.* New York: Macmillan.

"The Fruits of Free Trade: 2002 Annual Report." Federal Reserve Bank of Dallas, 2002, http://www.dallasfed.org/fed/annual/2002/ar02f.cfm.

Ghosh Roy, Atrayee. "Evidence on Economic Growth and Government Size." *Applied Economics,* 41, nos. 4–6 (February 2009): 607–14.

Gordon, John Steele. 2011. "A Short History of the Income Tax." *The Wall Street Journal,* September 27, 2011, section A.

Grossman, Gene M., and Elhanan Helpman. "Electoral Competition and Special Interest Politics." *Review of Economic Studies,* 63, no. 2 (1996): 265–86.

Hagenbaugh, Barbara. "More Home Buyers Go with Adjustable-Rate Mortgages." *USA Today,* March 30, 2005.

Hahn, Robert, and Caroline Cecot. 2007. "The Benefits and Costs of Ethanol" (Working paper 07-17). Washington, DC: AEI-Brookings Joint Center for Regulatory Studies.

Harberger, A. 1964. "Taxation, Resource Allocation, and Welfare." In *The Role of Direct and Indirect Taxes in the Federal Reserve System,* 25–80. Princeton, NJ: Princeton University Press.

Holbrook, T. M., and E. Vandunk. "Electoral Competition in the American States." *American Political Science Review,* 87, no. 4 (December 1993): 955–62.

Iacoviello, Matteo. 2011. "Housing Wealth and Consumption" (International Finance Discussion Paper No. 1027). Washington, DC: Federal Reserve System, Board of Governors.

Irwin, D. A. "The Smoot-Hawley Tariff: A Quantitative Assessment." *Review of Economics and Statistics,* 80, no. 2 (1998): 326–34.

Irwin, Douglas A. 2011. *Peddling Protectionism.* Princeton, NJ: Princeton University Press.

Kirkpatrick, David, and Duff Wilson. 2010. "One Grand Deal Too Many Cost Lobbyist His Job." *The New York Times,* February 12, 2010, Money and Policy section.

Kumar, M., and J. Woo. 2010. "Public Debt and Growth" (IMF Working Papers 1–47). Washington, DC: International Monetary Fund.

Miron, Jeffrey, and Katherine Waldock. 2010. "The Budgetary Impact of Ending Drug Prohibition." Washington, DC: Cato Institute.

Munnell, A. H., G. M. B. Tootell, L. E. Browne, and J. McEneaney. "Mortgage Lending in Boston: Interpreting HMDA Data." *The American Economic Review, 86,* no. 1 (1996): 25–53.

Owens, Emily. 2012. "The Birth of the Organized Crime? The American Temperance Movement and Market-Based Violence." Ithaca, NY: Cornell University. http://www.human.cornell.edu/pam/people/upload/Birth-of-the-Organized-Crime-Feb.pdf.

Passi, Peter. "DNT Investigation: Excelsior Lobbying Cash Questioned." *Duluth News Tribune,* September 12, 2011.

Pear, Robert. 2004. "House's Author of Drug Benefit Joins Lobbyists." *New York Times,* December 16, 2004, Washington section.

Reinhart, Carmen M., and Kenneth S. Rogoff. "Growth in a Time of Debt." *American Economic Review,* 100, no. 2 (2010): 573–78.

"Report Card on Effective Corporate Tax Rates." American Enterprise Institute, http://www.aei.org/outlook/101024.

"Richmond P. Hobson Argues for Prohibition." Schaffer Library of Drug Policy. http://www.druglibrary.org/schaffer/alcohol/hobson.htm.

Shiller, R. J. (2007). "Historic Turning Points" (Discussion Paper 1610). New Haven, CT: Cowles Foundation for Research in Economics.

Singer, Michelle. "Under the Influence." *60 Minutes,* February 11, 2009.

Steuerle, C. E., and Stephanie Rennane. 2011. "Social Security and Medicare Taxes and Benefits over a Lifetime." Washington, DC: Urban Institute. http://www.urban.org/publications/412281.html.

Thornton, Mark. 1991. "Alcohol Prohibition Was a Failure" (Policy Analysis No. 157). Washington, DC: *Cato Institute.*

Tynes, Sheryl R. 1996. *Turning Points in Social Security.* Stanford, CT: Stanford University Press.

Whaples, Robert. "Do Economists Agree on Anything? Yes!" *The Economists' Voice,* 3, no. 9 (2006). http://ew-econ.typepad.fr/articleAEAsurvey.pdf.

White, Lawrence H. 2012. "Monetary Policy and the Financial Crisis." In *Boom and Bust Banking: The Causes and Cures of the Great Recession.* Oakland, CA: The Independent Institute.

Wickersham Commission. 1931. *Report on the Enforcement of the of the Prohibition Laws of the United States.* http://www.druglibrary.org/schaffer/library/studies/wick/wick3.html.

Index

About the Author

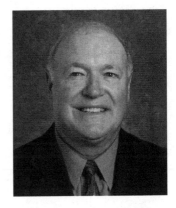

BURTON A. ABRAMS is Research Fellow at the Independent Institute, Director of the Institute's MyGovCost.org, and Professor of Economics at the University of Delaware.

Professor Abrams received his Ph.D. in economics from Ohio State University and has taught at the University of Split (Croatia), University of the Western Cape (South Africa), University of Adelaide, and Nankai University (China). He has also served as a visiting economist at the Federal Trade Commission and was a National Fellow at the Hoover Institution.

He is the author of *Return to Animal Farm* and *An Economic Theory of Lobbying: A Case Study of the U.S. Banking Industry*, and his articles and reviews have appeared in such scholarly journals as *Journal of Economic History*; *Public Choice*; *Eastern Economic Journal*; *Journal of Economic Perspectives*; *Southern Economic Journal*; *Journal of Money, Credit and Banking*; *Applied Economics*; *Journal of Economics and Business*; *Marine Resource Economics*; *National Tax Journal*; *Research in Law and Economics*; *Journal of Political Economy*; and *Journal of Broadcasting*. In addition, his popular articles have been published in the *Asian Wall Street Journal*, *Investor's Business Daily*, *Washington Times*, *Washington Examiner*, *Economic Exchange*, and *Reason*.

Independent Studies in Political Economy